A STUDY OF HOLINESS
FROM THE
EARLY CHURCH FATHERS

By

J. B. Galloway, B.S., Ph.B., B.D.

WIPF & STOCK · Eugene, Oregon

Wipf and Stock Publishers
199 W 8th Ave, Suite 3
Eugene, OR 97401

A Study of Holiness from the Early Church Fathers
By Galloway, J. B.
ISBN 13: 978-1-62564-521-0
Publication date 1/1/2014
Previously published by Beacon Hill Press, 1950

INTRODUCTION

Holiness Challenged

IF the teachings of the modern holiness movement are correct concerning the doctrine of holiness and the baptism with the Holy Ghost as an experience for the saints of God today perfecting them in Christian love and freeing them from carnal sin, it seems that we should find some evidences of this faith and teaching in the period of the history of the Church where it was the closest to the days of Christ. At least a germ of all truth should be evident when God planted the Church in the world. The Early Church before it had left its first love should show some traces of such an experience and doctrine. A careful study of this period of church history will show that the early Christians believed in holiness, and that an unbroken chain of witnesses has never ceased to give this great truth to the world. When we examine the writings of the first three hundred years of Christian history, we see that without doubt the Early Church believed in, practiced, and taught holiness. There was a diversity of opinions on some subjects, and sects arose that were not orthodox; yet we find much more on holiness than we would suppose could be found in the Primitive Church. They were in an age far from the intellectual light of modern times. Some of the doctrines of the Church had not been thought out very clearly; yet many of the writings of the best and holiest men of that day show clearly a trace of a belief in holiness. Few early writers do not contribute something to this great doctrine.

We do not say that the statements made in the early literature always mean the same that we would read into similar statements today. Detached expressions separated from the context may at times be misleading, and the translations may not always be exact; yet there is enough left after due allowance is made for all this to *show the light of holiness gleaming out from age to age where the saints of God served Him in truth.*

Realizing that this phase of the subject of holiness has not had very much study, the author has tried to make this work as exhaustive as possible. Years have been spent examining the literature of the Early Church. Between ten and fifteen thousand pages of the old writers have been tediously gone through from the writings of the Apostolic Fathers, Ante-Nicene literature, Apostolical Constitutions and Canons, apologies, homilies, liturgies, Apocryphal books, Biblical comments, and various other treatises, also old sermons, prayers, hymns, and the creeds from the Early Church. Also the ecclesiastical histories written before Constantine and the recent fragments that have come to light by modern archaeological research have not been overlooked. Most of the early literature has come down to us in the Greek or Latin tongue. Some has come in Hebrew, Syrian, and other languages, and some of this has not been translated. Where possible the author has used the original and the best translations obtainable that have appeared in England and America.

A CHALLENGE TO HOLINESS

The evidence is before you. Did the Early Church teach holiness? Is holiness a heritage of the whole Church? Every great crisis in Bible history was an effort on God's part to bring the world back to holiness; every great revival of religion contributed something to holy living.

It was the message of holiness that the fire-baptized disciples preached. It was the baptism with the Holy Spirit that made the martyr-age of the Church so glorious. Lactantius says:

> By reason of our strange and wonderful courage and strength new additions are made to us; for when people see men torn to pieces with infinite variety of torments, and yet maintain a patience unconquerable, and able to tire out their tormentors, they

begin to think (what the truth is) that the consent of so many, and the perseverance of the dying persons, cannot be in vain; nor that patience itself, were not from God, could not hold out under such racks and tortures. Thieves and men of robust bodies are not able to bear such tearing to pieces; they groan and cry out, and are overcome with pain, because not endured with divine patience; but our very women and children (to say nothing of men) do with silence conquer their tormentors; nor could the hottest fire force the least groan from them.

The places of martyrdom became such holy recruiting places where so many were converted to the hated faith that the Roman emperors were forced to forbid the public execution of the holy saints of God.

The young people of this generation have received from their fathers the clear, definite preaching of the doctrine of holiness. Will the children of the holiness movement be as faithful in giving this truth to the world and as consistent in living holy lives before all? They cannot afford to fail. Arise! On with the work of holiness until all have heard the message "holiness unto the Lord."

It is the message of the *Holy Bible*. Bishop Foster says:

> It breathes in the prophecy, thunders in the law, murmurs in the narrative, whispers in the promises, supplicates in the prayers, sparkles in the poetry, resounds in the songs, speaks in the types, glows in the imagery, voices in the language, and burns in the whole scheme, from the alpha to the omega, from its beginning to its end. Holiness! Holiness needed, holiness required, holiness offered, holiness attainable, holiness a present duty, a present privilege, a present enjoyment, is the progress and completeness of the wondrous theme.

It was the original intention of the author to give a study of holiness from the creeds of Christendom and holiness in other periods of church history, but space will make it necessary to use this in other works later.

CONTENTS

CHAPTER ONE

The Apostolic Fathers

THE FIRST LIGHT AFTER THE DAYS OF THE APOSTLES

AFTER the closing of the book of the New Testament it seems almost as if the Church had entered a dark tunnel of obscurity. The torch that had flamed forth from the hillsides of Judea was not eclipsed by the uncertainty of our knowledge of the history of those days, but it has continued to radiate its holy light to this day. We know very little of the history of the Church from the closing events of the Book of the Acts of the Apostles until the second decade of the next century. As we emerge from the shadows of the dark period following the days of the apostles, we find a number of writings which were written by the Apostolic Fathers. They were so-called because they immediately followed and were acquainted with the apostles. The earliest of these is Clement of Rome.

CLEMENT OF ROME AND HIS EPISTLE

Clement of Rome is the connecting link between the days of the apostles and the great stream of Christian writers which has continued unbroken from the second century. He has been identified with both the Clement mentioned by Paul in Philippians 4:3, and Flavius Clemens, a kinsman of Domitian, who was put to death by the latter for becoming a Christian. The ancient writer of the *Epistle of Clement* may be the person that Paul referred to; for Eusebius, the father of church history, places his death in A.D. 95, about thirty years after the time that Philippians was written. In the epistle itself St. Paul and St. Peter are mentioned together as men

"of our generation." Church history records that Clement
was the third bishop of Rome. He may be the writer of
this epistle. It is evident that Clement was a very great
man in the estimation of the Church. The fact that the
name of St. Clement was used in connection with the
many legends that have gathered around his life is a
proof of the great estimate in which he was held. Bishop
Lightfoot, by studying his epistle, came to the conclu-
sion that he was a Jewish Christian.

Two epistles are attributed to him. The first is universally received as genuine, but it seems certain that the
second is not his. The Shepherd of Hermas calls him
the author, and Hermas mentions that he knew him personally. The *Epistle of Clement* was written at Rome
and carried by three members of the church at Rome
to the church at Corinth. Its object was to exhort the
church at Corinth to unity. One or two persons had
started a schism and driven out the presbyters. The
trouble seems to have started over the question of re-
establishing the old ways that were vanishing from the
ministry.

CLEMENT OF ROME ON HOLINESS

In the days of John the Church was already leaving
its first love. Doubtless many, if not most, of those of
the church at Corinth were living holy lives, but he
would have them all united in this. He begins his epistle
as follows:

> The Church of God which is at Rome to the
> Church of God which is at Corinth, elect, sanctified,
> by the will of God, through Jesus Christ our Lord:
> grace and peace from the Almighty God, by Jesus
> Christ be multiplied unto you.

Effusion of Holy Ghost

In chapter two of the *Epistle of Clement* of Rome he
speaks of the Holy Ghost coming upon them.

Thus a firm, and blessed, and profitable peace was given unto you; and an unsatiable desire of doing good, and a plentiful effusion of the Holy Ghost.

Life of Holiness

In chapters twenty-nine and thirty he exhorts the Corinthians to a life of holiness thus:

Let us therefore come to Him with holiness of heart, lifting up chaste and undefiled hands unto Him; loving our gracious and merciful Father, who hath made us to partake of His election. . . . . Wherefore, we being the portion of the Holy One, let us do all these things that pertain unto holiness; fleeing all evil-speaking against one another.

Holiness Instead of Strife

Chapter forty-six is an exhortation for unity and holiness instead of division and strife.

Wherefore it will behoove us also, brethren, to follow such examples as these; for it is written, "Hold fast to such as are holy; for they that do so shall be sanctified." And again in another place He saith, "With the pure thou shalt be pure (and with the elect thou shalt be elect), but with the perverse man thou shalt be perverse." Let us therefore join ourselves to the innocent and righteous; for such as are elected of God. Wherefore are there strifes, and anger, and divisions, and schisms, and wars, among us? Have we not all one God and one Christ? Is not one spirit of grace poured out among us all? Have we not one calling in Christ? Why then do we rend and tear in pieces the members of Christ, and raise seditions against our own body: and are come to such a height of madness as to forget that we were members one of another? Remember the words of our Lord Jesus, how He said, "Woe to the man (by whom offences came)! It were better for him that he had never been born, than that he should have offended one of My elect. It were better for him that a millstone should be tied about his neck, and he cast into the sea, than that he should offend one of My little ones." Your schism has perverted many, has discouraged many; it has caused diffidence in many, and grief in us all.

Also chapter forty-eight is along the same line as the preceding.

Let us, therefore, with all haste, put an end to this sedition; and let us fall down before the Lord, and beseech Him with tears that He would be favorably reconciled to us, and restore us again to a seemly and holy course of brotherly love. For this is the gate of righteousness, opening unto life: as it is written, "Open unto me the gates of righteousness; I will go in unto them, and will praise the Lord. This is the gate of the Lord; the righteous shall enter into it." Although therefore many gates are opened, yet this gate of righteousness is that gate in Christ at which blessed are all they that enter in, and direct their ways in holiness and righteousness, doing all things without disorder. Let a man be faithful; let him be powerful in the utterance of knowledge; let him be wise in making an exact judgment of words; let him be pure in all his actions.

Perfect Love

He speaks of those who had the experience of perfect love, in chapter fifty.

All the ages of the world, from Adam to this day, are passed away; but they who have been made perfect in love have, by the grace of God, obtained a place among the righteous, and shall be made manifest in the judgment of the kingdom of Christ.

Just before closing his epistle, his soul cries out in prayer,

Guide thou our footsteps to walk in holiness and righteousness and singleness of heart, and to do all

—10—

things that are good and well-pleasing in Thy sight and the sight of our rulers. Yea, Lord, show Thy countenance upon us for good in peace, that we may be sheltered by Thy mighty hand and delivered from all sin by Thy lifted up arm, and deliver us from those who hate us unrighteously. Give oneness of mind and peace unto us and all those that dwell on the earth, as Thou didst give to our forefathers who called upon Thee in Holiness, in faith and truth (Chapter Sixty).

A Peculiar People

Now, God, the overseer of all things, the Father of spirits, and the Lord of all flesh—who hath chosen our Lord Jesus Christ, and us by Him to be a peculiar people—grant to every soul of man that calleth upon His glorious and holy name, faith, fear, peace, longsuffering, patience, temperance, holiness and sobriety, unto all well-pleasing in His sight; through our high priest and protector Jesus Christ, by Whom be glory, and majesty, and power, and honour, unto Him, now and forevermore. Amen.

IGNATIUS OF ANTIOCH AND HIS EPISTLES

The second name among the Apostolic Fathers is that of Ignatius. He was appointed the bishop of Antioch about the year A.D. 70. This is the city where the disciples of Christ were first called Christians. St. Paul started from here on his great missionary journeys, and planted the Cross in the cities of Asia Minor and Greece. Then we lose sight of the city until the days of Ignatius. Little is known of his life. He was probably a disciple of St. John, and an ancient tradition makes him the little child whom our Lord took up in His arms, when He told His disciples that they must become like little children if they would enter the kingdom of Heaven. This cannot be proved. He is described as:

A man in all things like unto the apostles, that as a good governor, by the helm of prayer and fasting, by the constancy of his doctrine and spiritual labour, he exposed himself to the floods of the adversary; that he was like a divine lamp illuminating the hearts of the faithful by his exposition of the Holy Scriptures; and lastly, that to preserve the church, he doubted not freely, and of his own accord, to expose himself to the most bitter death.

We are not certain how long he was bishop at Antioch. But persecution arose, and he was condemned to be killed by the wild beasts in the arena and for that purpose he was taken to Rome, under a guard of ten soldiers. On his way he was allowed the hospitality of the Christians but at times was treated very cruelly by the "ten leopards," the soldiers. During this journey he wrote many epistles to the churches: Ephesus, Magnesia, Tralles, Rome, Philadelphia, and Smyrnaean. Also he wrote to Polycarp, the Bishop of Smyrna. He suffered martyrdom between A.D. 107 and 117. The few bones that the wild beasts left were taken up by his friends and carried back to the city where he was bishop and were held as very precious jewels, and an annual festival was held in memory of him. Seven of his epistles are regarded as genuine; others are disputed.

HOLINESS IN THE EPISTLES OF IGNATIUS

Wholly Sanctified

From his *Epistle to the Ephesians,* chapter two, we read:

It is, therefore, fitting that you should by all means glorify Jesus Christ, who hath glorified you —that by a uniform obedience you should be perfectly joined together in the same mind, and in the same judgment, and may all speak the same things concerning every thing; and, that being subject to your bishop and the presbytery, ye may be wholly and thoroughly sanctified.

Full of Holiness

From the ninth chapter of the same epistle we quote:

As being the stones of the temple of the Father, prepared for His building, and drawn up on high by the cross of Christ as by an engine, using the Holy Ghost as the rope: your faith being your support, and your charity the way that leads unto God. Ye therefore, with all your companions in the same journey, full of God: His spiritual temples, full of Christ, full of holiness; adorned in all things with the commands of Christ.

No Herb of Devil

Chapter ten reads:

Pray also without ceasing for other men: for there is hope of repentance in them, that they may attain unto God. Let them, therefore, at least be instructed by your works, if they will in no other way. Be ye mild at their anger, humble at their boasting; to their blasphemies, return your prayers; to their error, your firmness in the faith: when they are cruel, be ye gentle; not endeavoring to imitate their ways: (let us be their brethren in all kindness and moderation, but let us be followers of the Lord: for whom was ever more unjustly used? more destitute? more despised?) that so no herb of the devil may be found in you; but ye may remain in all holiness and sobriety both of body and spirit, in Christ Jesus.

Faith and Charity

He shows that a believer lives above sin in chapter fourteen.

Of all which nothing is hid from you, if we have perfect faith and charity in Jesus Christ, which are the beginning and end of life; for the beginning is faith and the end is charity. And these two, joined together, are of God; but all other things which concern a holy life are the consequence of these, No man professing a true faith sinneth; neither does he who has charity hate any. The tree is made manifest by its fruit; so they who profess themselves to be Christians are known by what they do.

God's Temple

The last quotation from this epistle that we offer is from chapter fifteen.

He that possesses the word of Jesus is truly able to hear His very silence, that he may be perfect; and both do according to what He speaks, and be known by those things of which he is silent. There is nothing hid from God, but even our secrets are nigh unto Him. Let us do all things as becoming those who have God dwelling in them, that we may be His temple, and He may be our God.

Just before closing his *Epistle to the Magnesians*, Ignatius says: "Knowing you to be full of God, I have the more briefly exhorted you."

Wheat of God

Ignatius shows his devotion in time of trial and his courage in the face of martyrdom as he writes in his *Epistle to the Romans*.

I am willing to die for God, unless you hinder me. I beseech you that you show not an unseasonable good-will toward me. Suffer me to be the food of wild beasts, by whom I will attain unto God. For I am the wheat of God; and I will be ground by the teeth of the wild beasts, that I may be found the pure bread of Christ. .... Let fire and the cross; let companies of wild beasts; let breaking of bones and tearing of members; let the shattering in pieces of the whole body, and all the wicked torments of the devil come upon me; only let me enjoy Jesus Christ.

Christian Perfection

In chapter eleven of his *Epistle to the Smyrnaeans* he recognizes that there are those who have reached Christian perfection. He writes:

> For as much as ye are perfect yourselves, ye ought to think those things that are perfect. .... I would to God that all would imitate him [Burrhus], as a pattern of the ministry of God. . . . . Be strong in the power of the Holy Ghost.

The Martyrdom of Ignatius

From an ancient story of the martyrdom of St. Ignatius translated out of the original Greek in *Spicileg Patrum,* tome 2, we read an account of the trial and martyrdom of Ignatius. We quote the following:

> Trajan (the Roman Emperor)—"Dost thou carry Him who was crucified within thee?"
>
> Ignatius—"I do: for it is written, 'I will dwell in them.'" Then Trajan pronounced this sentence against him: "Forasmuch as Ignatius has confessed that he carries about within himself Him that was crucified, we command that he be carried, bound by soldiers, to the great Rome, there to be thrown to the beasts, for the entertainment of the people." When the holy martyr heard this sentence, he cried out with joy, "I thank Thee, O Lord, that Thou hast vouchsafed to honor me with a perfect love toward Thee."

Martyrs Perfected

The writer of this story tells how Ignatius was devoured by the wild beasts, except a few of the larger bones. And he says that he was an eyewitness to how this holy martyr perfected the course he had piously desired in Christ Jesus our Lord.

POLYCARP, A DISCIPLE OF SAINT JOHN

Polycarp was another one of the Apostolic Fathers. He was the bishop of Smyrna and one of the most celebrated of the early Christian martyrs. We have little information concerning his life. Such meager information as we have about his life is found in the writings of Irenaeus, Eusebius, and the anonymous *Martyrdom of Polycarp*. He was born about A.D. 69. As a youth he was acquainted with and later became a disciple of John. When Ignatius passed through Asia Minor on his way to Rome to be martyred he stopped and visited Polycarp, who was a bishop at that time. He afterwards addressed a letter to him. One of the last things that Polycarp did was to go to Rome to consult with the bishop there on the question of Easter. Soon after his return he was arrested by the Roman officers, tried on the charge of being a Christian, and condemned to death by burning. He was taken by the soldiers in a house near the city where he had taken refuge. He declined to avail himself of an opportunity to escape. When he was required to curse Christ, he answered: "Six and eighty years have I served Him, and He hath done nothing but good; and how could I curse Him, my Lord and my Saviour!" Refusing to renounce the faith, he was burned to death February 23, A.D. 155. such was the holiness of his life and such his heroism in martyrdom that he has been held ever since with the deepest veneration. He is said to have written several epistles, only one of which has come down to us.

Polycarp on Holiness

In Ignatius' *Epistle to Polycarp* he called him most holy Polycarp and exhorts him, "Stand firm and immovable as an anvil when it is beaten upon. It is the part of a brave combatant to be wounded, and yet to overcome." In Polycarp's *Epistle to the Philippians* he advises them to call to mind the doctrine which Paul taught them and exhorts all classes of Christians to holy living and Christian activities.

CHAPTER TWO

Irenaeus and the Beginning of the Church in Her Western Outposts

WITH Irenaeus we are introduced to the church in the West. For some time Christian missions had been flourishing on the banks of the Rhone. Polycarp sent Pthinus into Celtic Gaul. When he suffered death in the persecutions of Marcus Aurelius in A.D. 177, Irenaeus became the bishop of Ludgunum (Lyons, France). Irenaeus was born about A.D. 130, probably in Smyrna. As a youth he heard Polycarp, who was a disciple of the Apostle John. So he was just a step from the apostles. For a time he taught at Rome and then went to Gaul, where he became bishop of Lyons. He became one of the leading Church Fathers in the West. The remainder of his life was spent in the administration of his see. The bishop at Rome was trying to enforce uniformity in the Church on the paschal solemnities, and Irenaeus warned him that such a policy would rend the Church. His warning had the desired results. His greatest work was his *Against Heresies*. The full title of this work as he designated it was, *A Refutation and Subversion of Knowledge Falsely So-called*. This was written to combat the Gnostic teachings. He was well acquainted with these errors and answered them ably. There is much in the first part of his *Against Heresies* that is almost unintelligible and uninteresting to us, but in the last part of it there is much sound, valuable exposition of the Scriptures. Little is known about the last days of Irenaeus, but there is a fifth century tradition that he suffered martyrdom in the persecutions of Septimius Severus in A.D. 202.

In his *Against Heresies*, Book 4, chapter 16, in writing on perfect righteousness, he says:

> The Holy Spirit as a wise Artist uses circumcision as a sign of the work of the Spirit in our flesh. "For we have been counted," says the Apostle Paul, "all the day long as sheep for the slaughter"; that is consecrated to God, and administering continually to our faith and persevering in it, and abstaining from all avarice, and not acquiring treasures on earth.

Some Spiritual, Others Carnal

In Book 5, chapter 6, he shows that those who have the outpouring of the Spirit are the perfect and spiritual and that others are carnal.

> For this reason does the apostle declare, "We speak wisdom among them that are perfect," terming those persons perfect who have received the Spirit of God. In like manner we do hear many brethren in the church, who possess spiritual gifts, and who through the Spirit speak all kinds of languages, and bring to light for the general benefit hidden things of men, and declare the mysteries of God, whom also the apostles term spiritual, they being spiritual because they partake of the Spirit, and not because their flesh has been stripped off and taken away, and because they have become purely spiritual. For if anyone take away the substance of the flesh, that is, the handiwork of God, and understand that which is purely spiritual, such then would be a spiritual man, but would be the spirit of man, or the spirit of God. But when the spirit here blended with the soul is united to God's handiwork, the man is rendered spiritual and perfect because of the outpouring of the Spirit, and this is he who was made in the image and likeness of God. But if the Spirit be wanting to the soul, he who is such is indeed of an animal nature, and being carnal.

Preserved and Sanctified

Thus in the First Epistle of Thessalonians, "Now the God of peace sanctify you perfectly, and may your spirit, and soul, and body be preserved whole without complaint to the coming of the Lord Jesus Christ." Now what was the object in praying for these three—that is, the soul, body and spirit—might be preserved to the coming of the Lord, unless he was aware of the future reintegration and union of the three, and that they should be heirs of one and the same salvation? For this cause also he declares that those are perfect who present unto the Lord the three (component parts) without offence. These, then, are the perfect who have had the Spirit of God remaining in them, and have preserved their souls and bodies blameless, holding fast the faith of God, that is, that faith which is directed towards God, and maintaining righteous dealings with respect with their neighbors.

The Fruits of the Spirit

In Book 6, chapter 11, in treating the difference between the actions of the carnal and spiritual persons and showing that the cleansing of the Spirit is a spiritual one and not that of the flesh, he says:

And then again he [Paul in Gal. 5] proceeds to tell us of the spiritual actions which vivify a man, that is, the engrafting of the Spirit, thus saying, "But the fruit of the Spirit is love, joy, peace, longsuffering, goodness, benignity, faith, meekness, continence, chastity: against these there is no law." As, therefore, he who has gone forward to the better things, and hath brought forth the fruit of the Spirit, is saved altogether because of the communion of the Spirit; so also he who has continued in the works of the flesh, being truly reckoned carnal, because he did not receive the Spirit of God, shall not have power to inherit the kingdom of heaven.

CHAPTER THREE

Second Century Holiness Ideas

THE SHEPHERD OF HERMAS

Paul sent greetings to a Hermas at Rome (Rom. 16:14). It is uncertain whether this is the same person as the writer of the book of this discussion or not. Origen, Tertullian, Irenaeus, Eusebius, and other early writers say or seemingly imply that he was. Others place him a little later, sometime in the early part of the second century, contending that he was the brother of Pius, who was the bishop of Rome about A.D. 148.

The "Pilgrim's Progress" of the Early Church

The Shepherd of Hermas was one of the most popular books, if not the most popular, outside of the Scriptures that was read in the Early Church during the second, third, and fourth centuries. It has been compared to Bunyan's *Pilgrim's Progress*. Hermas had been a slave but was free in the time that he writes, according to the story. He was a married man and had children, but his domestic affairs were not the happiest. One day he met his former mistress and expressed a passing wish that he had a wife as handsome and good as she. Soon after she appeared to him again in a vision and reproached him for such evil thoughts. And other accusations were brought against him for not bringing up his children as he should, and not correcting and training them to repent. She then disappeared from the scene and an old woman symbolizing the Church appeared, and the scene shifted from Hermas and his family to the Church in general with its laxity and worldliness. Hermas was constrained to say that there was hope and pardon for those who had sinned after they were baptized. The rest of the book centers around the question of repentance. The book consists of three parts—four Visions, twelve Commandments, and ten Similitudes.

HERMAS ON HOLINESS

The book is somewhat curious but a story of some interest. From it we learn that the Christians of his day were thinking some on the question of holiness.

White Stones

From Book I, Vision 3, chapter 5, we read about the Church:

> Hear now then concerning the stones that are in the building. The square and white stones, which agree exactly in their joints, are the apostles, and bishops and doctors, and ministers, who through the mercy of God have come in, and governed and taught, and ministered holily and modestly to the elect of God.

Holiness Required

In chapter 7 we read:

> They are such as have heard the word, and were willing to be baptized in the name of the Lord, but, considering the great holiness which the truth requires, have withdrawn themselves, and walked again after their wicked lusts.

In chapter 9 we read:

> Hear me, therefore, O my sons! I have bred you up in much simplicity, and innocency, and modesty, for the mercy of God, which was dripping down upon you in righteousness; that you should be sanctified.

Full of Joy

From Book II, the second command, we read:

> Put on a holy constancy, in which there are no sins, but all is full of joy; and do good of thy labors.

Take Heed to Thyself

From Book III, the fifth similitude, chapter three, we read:

Take heed to thyself, and keep thyself from every wicked act, and from every filthy word, and from hurtful desire; and purify thy mind from all the vanity of this present world.

In chapter six, we read:

For every pure body shall receive its reward, that is found without spot, in which the Holy Spirit has been appointed to dwell.

In chapter seven, we read:

Thou shalt not defile thy body and spirit; for they are companions together, and the one cannot be defiled, and the other will be so too. Keep, therefore, both of them pure, and thou shalt live unto God.

From the ninth similitude, chapter thirteen, we read:

So shall a man in vain bear His name, unless he shall be endued with power.

Purify Thy House

In the tenth similitude, chapter three, the Christian virtues are likened to virgins, and we read:

Only do thou purify thy house; for they shall readily dwell in a clean house. For they are clean, and chaste, and industrious; and all of them have grace with the Lord. If therefore, thou shalt have thy house pure, they will abide with thee; but if it shall be never so little polluted, they will immediately depart from thy house; for the virgins cannot endure any manner of pollution.

From this story in symbolical pictures we see what was taught and expected in the Church of the second century.

BARNABAS AND HIS EPISTLE

The question naturally arises, Is the author of the *Epistle of Barnabas* the Barnabas that we read about in the Book of the Acts of the Apostles? Clement of Alexandria, Origen, Eusebius, and Jerome of the early centuries say that he was. It is evident that this epistle does not belong to the inspired Scriptures even though it is written by a Christian mentioned in the New Testament. There are some passages of great spiritual beauty and eloquence; yet it abounds in foolish and trivial allegories. The *Epistle* was written soon after the fall of Jerusalem to show the Jewish Christians that the old dispensation and worship was a shadow of the Christian. It may be that it served a temporary purpose God designed, yet is far inferior to the inspired Scriptures. Yet we cannot be sure that the Barnabas of the New Testament is its author.

THE EPISTLE OF BARNABAS ON HOLINESS

A Perfect Temple

From section four we read:

Let us become spiritual, a perfect temple to God. As much as in us lies, let us meditate upon the fear of God; and strive, to the utmost of our power, to keep His commandments, that we may rejoice in His righteous judgments.

Milk and Honey

From section six we read:

Enter ye into the land flowing with milk and honey, and have dominion over it. Wherefore ye see how we were again formed anew; as also He speaks; by another prophet, "Behold, saith the Lord, I will take from them (that is, those whom the Spirit of the Lord foresaw) their hearts of stone, and will put in them hearts of flesh"; because He was about to be made manifest in the flesh, and to dwell in us. For, my brethren, the habitation of our heart is a holy temple unto the Lord.

Clean Hands and Pure Hearts

From section sixteen we read how to keep the Sabbath:

Thou shalt sanctify it with clean hands, and a pure heart. Therefore we are greatly deceived if we imagine that anyone can now sanctify that day which God has made holy, without having a heart pure in all things. Behold, therefore He will then truly sanctify it with blessed rest, when we having received the righteous promise, when iniquity shall be no more, all things being renewed by the Lord shall be able to sanctify it, being ourselves first made holy.

THEOPHILUS OF ANTIOCH

Little is known of the personal history of Theophilus of Antioch. He was born about A.D. 115, just a short time after the death of John the apostle. We would gather from his own writings that he was born a pagan and converted to Christianity by reading the Holy Scriptures. From the *Ecclesiastical History* of Eusebius we learn that he became bishop of Antioch in A.D. 168, and that he was the sixth bishop of Antioch of Syria. He was content to be called, "Nothing but a Christian." Ancient authors say that he wrote several treatises, several of them against heresies of his day. He comes down to us as an apologist; he was severe, yet gentle in dealing with his antagonists. He is one of the earliest commentators on the Gospels, if not the first; he arranged them in the form of a harmony. But all that remains of his writings are his three books addressed to Autolycus. The occasion that brought them forth is doubtful, but it is thought that they were in answer to works written against Christianity. He is fond of fanciful interpretations of scripture, but has a profound knowledge of the Holy Scriptures. He shows the superiority of Christianity over the heathen religions, and his works would make a very favorable impression for Christianity. He died about A.D. 181.

THEOPHILUS ON HOLINESS

In Book I, chapter 13, of his *To Autolycus*, writing on the meaning of the word Christian, he says that it is derived from a word meaning to anoint.

Anointed

Thus the early believers were called Christians because they were anointed with the Spirit. He says that no ship is serviceable or seaworthy which has not been anointed, and the man that goes to the gymnasium is first anointed with oil, and therefore, "We are called Christians on account of this fact, because we are anointed with the oil of God"—not the material oil, but the anointing of the Holy Ghost (I John 2:20). The argument of this chapter depends upon the literal meaning of the word Christos—Christ, the Anointed One.

Possessed

In Book III, chapter 17, we have this sentence, "How much more, then, shall we know the truth who are instructed by the holy prophets, who were possessed by the Holy Spirit of God." Here he recognizes the fact that saints may be, and some have been, possessed by the Holy Spirit.

ARISTIDES, THE PHILOSOPHER

Church historians declare him to be the first of the lost apologists. Several of the early writers mention his work, but it has been lost until recently. He was a Christian philosopher of Athens; he is mentioned by Eusebius as a contemporary with Quardratus, who lived so near to the lifetime of Christ that he declares some who had been healed by Christ "lived on to our times." He must have been a boy when the Apostle John died. His *Apology* was written between A.D. 124 and 140. It is addressed to the Emperor Hadrian.

In 1889 Professor J. Rendel Harris had the honor of finding a Syrian translation of the long-lost *Apology of Aristides* in one of the libraries of the Convent of St. Catherene, on Mount Sinai. In looking over some Greek manuscripts which were thrown indiscriminately into large chests, the librarian was interested enough to take him to another part of the convent where a door closed by a rusty padlock was thrown open and a narrow room was reached, whose walls were lined with old books in the Syriac, Arabic, and Iberian languages.

There is a seventh century book which is claimed to be the work of John of Damascus that contains the *Apology of Aristides*. It was very popular and was translated into many languages. As early as 1204, the King of Norway had it translated into Icelandic. The story is as follows:

> A king of India, Abennar, was an enemy to the Christians. He had an only son Josaphat. At his birth the astrologers predicted that he would become great and embrace a new religion. His father did all he could to prevent him from doing this. But seeing the misery about him he visited a Christian hermit—Barlaam by name—and was converted to Christianity. To undo this, his father arranged a discussion held by one of the king's sages, Machor, who was to make a very weak statement of the Christian case. But when the day comes he begins, "like Balaam's beast spake words that he did not intend to use," and he quoted the *Apology of Aristides*. He converts himself, the king, and all the people.

The *Apology of Aristides* is a bold challenge to the heathen emperor showing the superior moral character of the Christians, the modesty of the women, their kindness to the poor, their assurance in prayer, and their joy in death.

Aristides on Holiness

In describing the Christians in the Greek manuscript, he says in chapter 15, "And they are ready to sacrifice their lives for the sake of Christ; for they observe His commandments without swerving, and live holy and just lives, as the Lord God enjoined upon them." The Syrian version varies a little in the statements.

CHAPTER FOUR

Clement of Alexandria

A LINK IN THE EARLY CHRISTIAN SCHOOLS

HIS full name was Titus Flavius Clemens. He was a celebrated Greek father of the Early Church, of about A.D. 153 to 217. It is uncertain whether he was born in Alexandria, Egypt, or Athens. He was probably born of heathen parents and received a liberal education and sought many teachers; for this purpose he traveled extensively through Greece, Italy, Egypt, Palestine, and the East. He finally resorted to Pantænus, who presided over the Christian school at Alexandria. Here he entered the Church and was made a presbyter. He taught with great distinction and succeeded Pantænus as the head of this famous school. During the persecution of Septimius Severus he left Egypt, and later we hear of him in Palestine and Asia Minor. His last days are veiled with obscurity, so that we do not know the place or time of his death. He was followed in the school by his pupil Origen. Clement of Alexandria was a man of great learning and proficient in Greek philosophy, literature, and history.

His greatest works are: *Exhortation to the Heathen*, the object of which was to win them to the Christian faith; the *Instructor*, which contains instruction in morals and matters of everyday life; and the *Stromata*, which is a miscellaneous collection of unsystematic discussions of doctrinal points. In these he tries to guide the mature Christian to perfect knowledge.

He speaks of a young man's being baptized and then anointed with oil. After the Church began to anoint the young converts with oil, they would pray that they might be filled with the Holy Ghost. The anointing was called sealing; this was probably from Ephesians 1:13 (see Eusebius, Book III, chapter 17).

CLEMENT OF ALEXANDRIA ON HOLINESS

Free from All Sin

He believed that a man could be freed from all sin, but thought that it would be done at baptism. In his *Instructor,* Book I, chapter 6, he says:

> Thus also we who are baptized, have wiped off the sins which obscure the light of the divine Spirit, and have the eye of the Spirit free and unimpaired, full of light, by which we contemplate the divine, the Holy Spirit flowing down from above. This is the eternal adjustment of vision, which is able to see the eternal light, since like loves like; and that which is holy loves that from which holiness proceeds, which has appropriately been termed light.

Still Carnal

A little further on in the chapter he sees a distinction between the spiritual and the carnal Christian, for he says:

> For he called those who had already believed, spiritual, and those newly instructed and not yet purified, carnal, whom with justice he calls still carnal, as minding equally with the heathen the things of the flesh.

Perfect Women

In Book 4, chapter 19, he shows that woman is capable of perfection as well as man. In chapters 20 and 21 he gives a description of the perfect man. "Who then is perfect? He who professes abstinence from what is bad." He shows that the Spirit distributes the gifts of the Spirit that each may be perfect in his own place of service.

—28—

And the same Spirit, distributing to each according to His will. Such being the case, the prophets are perfect in prophecy, the righteous in righteousness, the martyrs in confession, and others in preaching, not that they are not sharers in the common virtues, but are proficient in those to which they are appointed.

Holy Thoughts

In chapter 22 he says:

We ought to go washed to the sacrifices and prayers, clean and bright; that this external adornment and purification are practiced for a sign. Now purity is to think holy thoughts . . . . For purity, as I conceive it, is perfect pureness in mind, and deeds and thoughts, and words too.

Dignified with the Spirit

In chapter 25 he shows that true perfection consists in the knowledge of the love of God, and in chapter 26 he shows how the perfect man treats the body and the things of the world. He says:

. . . . that those who run down created existence and vilify the body are wrong . . . . Whence this abode becomes receptive of the soul which is most precious to God; and is dignified with the Holy Spirit through the sanctification of soul and body, perfected with the perfection of the Saviour . . . . The body too, is one sent on a distant pilgrimage, using inns and dwellings by the way, caring for the things by the way, of the place where he halts; but leaving his dwelling and property without excessive emotion, ... giving thanks for the sojourn, and blessing God for his departure, embracing the mansion in heaven.

Holy Builders

In his *Stromata*, Book 7, chapter 5, he shows that a holy soul is a more excellent temple than any man-made edifice. He begins by saying:

For is it not the case that rightly and truly we do not circumscribe in any place that which cannot be circumscribed; nor do we shut up in temples made with hands that which contains all things? What work of builders, and stone-cutters, and mechanical art can be holy?

Holy Altar of Prayer

In the next chapter we read that prayer and praise from a pure mind is better than sacrifices.

But if, by nature needing nothing, He delights to be honored, it is not without reason that we honor God in prayer; and thus the best and holiest sacrifice with righteousness we bring, presenting it as an offering to the most righteous Word, by whom we receive knowledge, giving glory to Him for that we have learned.

A little farther on he says,

And will they not believe us when we say that the righteous soul is the truly sacred altar, and the incense arising from it is holy prayer?

Steps to Perfection

In chapter 10 he gives the steps to perfection, and begins with knowledge.

For knowledge to speak generally, a perfecting of man as man, is consummated by acquaintance with divine things, in character, life, and word, accordant and conformable to itself and to the divine Word. For by it faith is perfected, inasmuch as it is solely by that the believer becomes perfect. Faith is an internal good, and without searching for God, confesses His existence, and glorifies Him as existent.

Commenting further on faith, he says:

And this takes place when one hangs on the Lord by faith, by knowledge, by love, and ascends along with Him to where the God and guard of our faith is . . . . It leads us to an endless and perfect end, teaching us beforehand the future life, that we shall lead, according to God.

Again he says in the same chapter,

After which redemption the rewards and honors are assigned to those who have become perfect; when they have done with purification, and cease from all service, though it be holy service.

Society of Angels

In chapter 12 he says of a holy man:

His whole life is prayer and converse with God. And if he be pure from sins, he will by all means obtain what he wishes. For He says to the right-eous man, "Ask, and I will give thee." . . . . So he is always pure for prayer. He also prays in the society of angels, as being already of angelic rank, and he is never out of their holy keeping; and though he pray alone, he has the choir of saints standing around him.

We will close with a statement from chapter 12. Here he is commenting upon I Corinthians 6:1, and he says of a holy man:

But ye are sanctified, for he who has come to this state is in a condition to be holy, falling in none of the passions in any way, but as it were separated and already grown holy without this earth.

CHAPTER FIVE

Tertullian, the Chief of the Latin Apologists

TERTULLIAN, THE CHRISTIAN DEFENDER

He was born at Carthage in North Africa, probably of pagan parents. He was the son of a proconsular centurion. He was well educated, especially in Roman law. His birth is placed at about A.D. 145. Attracted by the courage of the Christians, he was converted and used his great literary gifts for the Church. He was a married man and wrote treatises addressed to his wife. He was a presbyter until middle age, and later in life espoused the party of Montanus. Persecution was prevalent during the early part of his life but he escaped, in spite of his vigorous protests against the persecutors. His chief service to the Church was that of a Christian defender, which he did with great zeal, and was not interrupted until death. No early father is more valuable to us than Tertullian, for the vivid pictures he gives us of both pagan and Christian life.

Tertullian, the Montanist

His fierce temperament led him always to extremes, and in middle life he joined the Montanists, finding their rigid asceticism and spiritual enthusiasm more congenial than the ordinary life of the Church, which was beginning to drift away from the truth. His doctrine, however, is strictly orthodox, and he is the father of Latin theology. Such words as Trinity, substance, person, sacrament, and church as used for a building occur first in their Latin form in his writings.

The Montanists arose in Asia Minor in the century. They were eminently spiritual people, and bitterly persecuted. They became a separate sect in the third century and were expelled by Rome, for they stood by the old paths against the Catholic hierarchal tendency. They insisted upon regeneration followed by heart purity with the baptism of the Holy Ghost, which they professed to enjoy. They contended for Christian perfection and a pure, spotless Church; fasted frequently, prayed much, testified with joy; gave freedom to the Holy Ghost, and shouted in their worship. They insisted upon a divine call to preach. They forbade all ornamentation in clothing and the appearance of their women in immodest attire. They looked with contempt upon this present world, living under a vivid impression of the great final catastrophe, believing that Christ would come and reign personally during the millennium. They were ardent believers in the second advent of Christ, which they believed near at hand. John Wesley says of Montanus, their founder, that "he was not only a truly good man, but one of the best men then on the earth."

Tertullian, the Writer

He was the first great Latin writer in the Church. Even at Rome the language of the Church was Greek to the end of the second century. His writings include several apologetic works, more bitter in tone than the Greek apologists; a long doctrinal work *Against Marcion* (the most formidable heretic who had yet opposed the Christians); and many ethical and theological essays. His *Apology Against the Pagans*, written about A.D. 197, is the most brilliant defensive writing in the Early Church. It is a masterpiece in unity and skill. He shows the unjustness of persecution, and proves the error of the charges against the Christians. He proves the unity of God in his *Proof of the Soul* and *Against the Heathen Mythology*. He wrote a book to the proconsul Scapula, who was very cruel to the Christians. He answered the

Jewish arguments in his book *Against the Jews,* and proves the immortality of man in his book on *The Resurrection.*

TERTULLIAN ON HOLINESS

The early Christian writers say that it was customary in the second century and afterward to pray for the Christians to be filled with the Spirit. From Tertullian we learn that it was the practice to anoint the baptized believer with oil before praying that he be filled with the Holy Ghost. Oil was used as a symbol of the Spirit. Kings and priests were anointed with oil in the Old Testament, and the sick were anointed in the New Testament for healing. As water in baptism symbolized cleansing from sin, so the anointing with oil symbolized the baptism of the Spirit.

Inviting the Holy Spirit

In Tertullian's *On Baptism,* chapter 8, he says: "In the next place the hand is laid on us invoking and inviting the Holy Spirit through benediction." Further on, "Then over our cleansed and blessed bodies willingly descends from the Father the holiest Spirit." In chapter 10 of the same book we read, "And so the baptism of repentance was dealt with as if it were a candidate for sanctification shortly about to follow Christ."

Sanctified by the Holy One

Water was looked upon as a chosen vehicle of divine operation, a type of cleansing. In chapter 4 we read:

By the very attitude assumed for a type of baptism, that the Spirit of God, who hovered over the waters from the beginning, would continue to linger over the waters of the baptized. But a holy thing, of course hovers over a holy; or else, from that which was hovered over borroweth a holiness, since it is necessary that in every case an underlying substance should catch the quality of that which overhangs it. . . . . Thus the nature of the waters, sanctified by the Holy One, itself conceived the power of sanctifying.

Not so clear on how you get holiness, but expecting it.

Gifts of the Spirit

In *Against Marcion*, Book I, chapter 28, Tertullian shows that if Marcion is right the sacraments have no virtue, and there would be no need for regeneration, nor the gift of the Spirit. His words are:

> If the regeneration of man, how can he regenerate that which has never been generated? If the bestowal of the Holy Ghost, how will he bestow the Spirit, who did not at first impart life? For the life is in a sense the supplement of the Spirit. He therefore seals men, who have never been unsealed in respect of him; washed men who had never been defiled so far as he was concerned . . . . Why then impose sanctity upon our most infirm and unworthy flesh, either as a burden or as a glory? What shall I say, too, of the uselessness of a discipline which sanctifies what is already sanctified? . . . . Why keep back from a work its due reward?

In Book V, chapter 8, he has a long chapter discussing the gifts of the Spirit, comparing the prophets' prophecy and the apostles' declaration fulfillment, and challenging Marcion to produce anything like the gifts of the Spirit foretold by the prophets.

Illumination of the Spirit

He shows the need of being filled with the Spirit. In *On the Resurrection of the Flesh,* he says:

> The flesh is washed, that the soul may be cleansed; the flesh is anointed, that the soul may be consecrated; the flesh is signed or sealed, that the soul may be fortified; the flesh is overshadowed with the imposing of hands, that the soul may be illuminated by the Spirit.

The Old and the New Man

In chapter 45 of the same book he explains the old man and new man in Paul's epistles. And in chapter 46 he shows that it is the work of the flesh and not the bodily flesh itself that is carnal and sinful. A quotation reads:

> In like manner he [the apostle] called "the carnal mind" first "death," and afterwards "enmity against God"; but he never predicated this against the flesh itself. But to what then, you will say, must the carnal mind be ascribed, if it is not to the carnal substance itself? I will allow your objection, if you will prove that the flesh has any discernment of its own. If however, it has no conception of anything without the soul, you must understand that the carnal mind must be referred to the soul, although ascribed sometimes to the flesh, on the grounds that it is ministered for the flesh and through the flesh. And therefore the apostle says that "sin dwelleth in the flesh," because the soul by which sin is provoked has its temporary lodging in the flesh, which is doomed indeed to death, not however on its own account, but on account of sin.

Christian Modesty

He is very strong in his arguments against worldliness. He covers almost every phase of dress and conduct in his two books *On the Apparel of Women*. He begins Book I, chapter 1, by saying:

> If there dwell upon earth a faith as great as the reward which is expected in heaven, no one at all, beloved sisters, from the time she first knew the Lord, and learned the truth concerning her own condition, would have a desire to gladsome (not to say too ostentatious) a style of dress.

He says perfect modesty will abstain from everything that tends to sin. In Book II, chapter 2, we read:

You must know that in the eye of perfect, that is Christian modesty, carnal desire of one's self on the part of others, is not only not to be desired or even expected of you: first, because the study of personal grace as a means of pleasing does not spring from a sound conscience. Why therefore excite towards yourself that evil passion? Why invite that to which you profess your self a stranger? Second, because we ought not to open a way to temptation, which by their instancy sometimes achieves wickedness which God expels from those who are His. We ought indeed to walk so holily, and with so entire substantiality of faith to be confident and secure in regard to our conscience.

CHAPTER SIX

In the Fires of Persecution

THE STORY OF PERPETUA AND FELICITAS

(Condensed from what is claimed to be the story begun by Perpetua herself and finished by Tertullian, an eyewitness.—J. B. G.)

This beautiful story comes from the second century and begins as follows:

> If ancient illustrations of faith which both testify to God's grace and tend to man's edification are collected in writing, so by the perusal of them, as if by that reproduction of the facts, as well God may be honored, as man may be strengthened; why should not new instances be collected, that should be equally suitable for such purposes?

Chapter 1. The Young Christians Thrust into a Dungeon

Five young catechumens from among the early Christians were apprehended. They were Saturnias, Secundulas, Revocatus, Felicitas, and Perpetua. The last two mentioned were respectable, educated, married young women. Perpetua had a father, mother, and two brothers, one of whom was a catechumen like herself. She was twenty-two years of age and had an infant son at her breast. While she was being taught the way of the Christians, her father tried to persuade her away from her faith, but she said to him, "Father, do you see this little vessel lying here to be a pitcher?" And he said, "I see it to be." And she answered him, "Can it be called by any other name but a pitcher?" He said, "No." "Neither can I be called anything else than what I am, a Christian."

This provoked her father and he rushed toward her as if he would tear her eyes out. But he only distressed her and went away, and the Lord became a source of consolation to her. After a few days she was baptized, and shortly afterwards she was taken to the dungeon by her enemies with her fellow Christians. At first she was much frightened by the terrible darkness, the great heat, the soldiers, and the mob about her; and unusually disturbed for her infant. Christian friends came and ministered to her, arranged for some comforts, and brought to her her babe that was becoming feeble by hunger. Such solicitude she suffered many days, and her child was allowed to remain with her; and she says, "Forthwith I became strong and the dungeon became to me as it were a palace."

Soon afterwards her brother came to her and said, "You are already highly honored, and you may ask a vision that it may be known to you whether you are to be martyred or released." She said, "I will let you know tomorrow."

In the meanwhile she saw a golden ladder of marvelous height reaching up to heaven, so that anyone could ascend up to heaven on it one by one. There were swords, lances, hooks, and daggers; so that if anyone went up carelessly he would be torn, and caught on the cruel weapons of iron. A great and dreadful dragon was at the bottom to frighten anyone who would ascend away. Saturnias ascended to the top and cried to her, "Perpetua, I am waiting for you, but be careful that the dragon does not get you." Then she went up into a beautiful garden and saw a shepherd at the gate, who said, "Thou art welcome." And he gave her a little cake and she ate it, and all about her said, "Amen." When she told this to her brother and friends, they realized that she was to be martyred.

Chapter 2. *Perpetua Avows Herself a Christian and Is Condemned with Her Fellow Christians to the Wild Beasts*

A few days after her father heard the report, and he came to her and tried to persuade her away from the Christians. He said, "Have pity, my daughter, on my gray hairs. Have pity on thy father. With my own hands have I brought thee up to this, the flower of thy age. I have preferred thee above all thy brothers. Have regard for thy brothers, thy mother and aunts. Have regard for thy infant son, who will not be able to live without thee. Do not bring this destruction upon us all." These things said her father, and affectionately kissed her hands, throwing himself at her feet in bitter tears. She comforted him and said, "Whatever God wills shall happen." Then he departed in sorrow.

Sometime afterwards while she was at dinner she heard a great noise, and saw that great crowds were gathering to the town hall. At once a rumor spread through the neighborhood that the Christians were to be taken to the court platform and interrogated. She saw an immense crowd of people gathering. When she stepped out for the trial she saw her father with her little boy, and he tried to persuade her against the Christians, saying, "Have mercy upon thy child."

And Hilarianus, who had just received the power of life and death as a proconsul, said, "Spare the gray hairs of your father; spare thy son. Offer up sacrifices for the honor of the emperor." And she replied, "I will not do so." Hilarianus asked, "Are you a Christian?" And she said, "I am a Christian." Then her father tried to lead her from the platform, but he was ordered to be cast down and beaten with rods. She was greatly grieved for her father's misfortune and suffering, for he was old and feeble. Then the proconsul delivered judgment upon all the Christians, and pronounced that all should be condemned to the wild beasts. She sent and asked her father that her infant son might remain with her, but he would not. While she yet remained in fetters, she had a vision of her brother who years ago, when he was seven years old, died. He appeared to her as bright and beautiful, and drinking from a vessel filled to the brim.

Chapter 3. Perpetua Has Further Trials and Visions

After a few days Prudens, a soldier overseer of the prison, who had regard for and held her in high esteem, perceived that God was with her, and admitted her Christian friends to see her. As the day of her execution drew nigh, her father, worn with suffering, came again to her, and began to tear his beard, and throw himself to the ground, and reproach himself in such words that would move a heart of stone. She was greatly grieved.

The day before her execution she saw in a vision Pomponius, the deacon, come to her and knock at her door. He was clothed in a richly ornamented robe of white. He said to her, "Perpetua, we are waiting for you to come!" And he reached out his hand to help her over the rough places. When they reached the amphitheater, he led her breathlessly into the arena. Then he said, "Do not fear; I am with you," and disappeared. She marveled that the wild beasts did not appear; but soon she saw an Egyptian, terrible in appearance, come out to fight with her with backers. Then there came helpers to her and she seemed to be transformed into a soldier. Also she saw the tall trainer of the gladiators; he wore a loose tunic and had a purple robe between bands over his breast, and he carried a rod and a green branch upon which were apples of gold; who said, "If this Egyptian overcome this woman he shall be killed with a sword, and if she conquer she shall have this branch." They drew near together and began to deal out blows. She was victorious, and he fell upon his face. The branch was given to her and the people shouted and said, "Daughter, peace be unto thee." When she awoke she understood that her great fight was with Satan rather than the beasts.

Then Saturnias told his vision to Perpetua. He said he saw four angels floating upward, and they bore Perpetua through space to the pleasure-gardens where were roses of every kind blossoming. They were as tall as a cypress and leaves were falling incessantly. Other four angels, brighter than the previous ones, appeared; and they said to the rest of the angels, "Here they are! Here they are!" And the walls of the place were such as were built of light, and before the gates stood angels clothed in white robes, and their united voices said, "Holy! Holy! Holy!" And also he saw one in the midst with snowlike hair, and on his right hand and on his left were twenty-four elders. The elders said, "Go in and enjoy. Perpetua, you have your wish." All were nourished with an indescribable odor which satisfied all. And then he awoke.

Chapter 4. The Arena and the Crown of Glory

The day of their victory shone forth brightly. The Christians proceeded from the prison cells into the amphitheater, as to an assembly, joyous and of brilliant countenances, with joy and without shrinking or fear. To Felicitas had been born a child just recently; yet she rejoiced that she was able to go forth with the other Christians to die for her faith. When they were brought to the gate the men were constrained to put on the garments of the priests of Saturn, and the women that which was consecrated to Ceres. Felicitas said, "We have thus far come of our own accord. And it has been agreed with you that we should come thus." So they were allowed to enter as they were. Then Perpetua sang psalms. When they came into sight of Hilarianus, the proconsul, Revocatus and Saturnias said of him, "Thou judgest us, but God will judge thee." To this the people shouted in exasperation that they should be tortured with scourges as they passed along the ranks. They rejoiced that they should thus suffer for the Lord.

Saturnias was thrown to the wild beasts. Revocatus was harassed by the bear and the leopard. But Saturnias was recalled unhurt. Then the wild boar was called and would not be enticed from his den; so he was recalled again.

When the young women were called, their enemies prepared a very fierce cow. So they were clothed in nets and led forth. The crowd shuddered when they saw these two young mothers, delicate and led away from their infants. Perpetua was led into the arena first. She was tossed and fell upon her side. When she saw that her garments were torn she wrapped them about her. She was called forth again and bound up her disheveled hair. This time as she raised up she saw Felicitas crushed. So she approached her and gave her her hand, and lifted her up; both stood together. Then Perpetua, as roused from sleep, being so much in the Spirit that she did not realize what had happened until she saw the signs of it in her body and garments; then she recognized another Christian addressing her, saying, "Stand fast in the faith."

At the same moment Saturnias, entering again, exhorted Prudens, the friendly soldier, saying, "Up to this moment I have felt no hurt, now believe with the whole heart. Lo, I am going forth to the beasts. I shall be destroyed with one bite." Prudens desired a token dipped in his blood, and he said to him, "Farewell, be mindful of thy faith." Thus the vision of Perpetua, that she saw of Saturnias ascending the ladder before her and waiting in spirit until she came, was fulfilled. But Perpetua, when she felt the pain of the sword, waved her hand to the youthful gladiator. Thus the brave martyrs entered in and took the crowns for their faith!

CHAPTER SEVEN

Origen, the Father of Bible Interpretation

THE greatest Bible scholar of the Early Church was Origen, surnamed Adamantius, born at Alexandria, about the year A.D. 185. He was one of the greatest of all Christian thinkers. The Church is forever indebted to him for his encyclopedic labors on the Scriptures in producing the *Hexapla*. He was born in a Christian home. His father was a teacher of rhetoric and grammar and a man of decided piety. Under his superintendence, the youthful Origen was educated in all the Grecian knowledge and also required daily to memorize a portion of scripture. The spirit of inquiry into the meaning of the Scriptures showed itself early. He was never satisfied with the plain meaning of them, but sought to penetrate into the deeper meaning of them. His father Leonidas rebuked him for his curiosity, but rejoiced to himself at the signs of genius that he saw in his son, and thanked God for being permitted to be the father of such a child. He would imprint kisses on the breast of the child while he was sleeping and say, "The temple of the Holy Ghost."

When Origen was seventeen years old, his father was martyred in the persecution of Septimius Severus. He wrote to his father while he was in prison, exhorting him to constancy under trials. He wished to share the same fate as his father, but was prevented from leaving home by his mother's hiding his clothes. At the death of his father their property was confiscated, and he was left with his mother and six younger brothers to support. A wealthy lady opened her home to him a short time; but, finding his position here uncomfortable, he resolved to enter the career of a teacher to support himself.

His careful instruction by his father in the Grecian literature, and his own diligence and ability, speedily attracted attention and brought him many pupils; some of these sought to be instructed in the principles of the Christian religion. Bishop Demetrius appointed him as a master in the Catechetical School. A youth not yet past eighteen years took the place of Clement, who had retired because of persecution. He refused remuneration, and lived upon a scanty pittance, laboring in the school by day and studying the Scriptures the greater part of the night.

On a visit to Cæsarea he was allowed by the bishop to expound the Scriptures in church, while yet a layman. This aroused the jealousy of the Bishop of Alexandria, who ordered him to return. A short time afterward he was forbidden to teach at Alexandria and excommunicated. He went to Cæsarea and was honorably received, admitted to the priesthood, and allowed to work for more than twenty years.

Ambrose, a man of large means, had a great admiration for Origen and was delighted to bear the expense of having his works transcribed and published. He furnished him with "more than seven amanuenses and an equal number of transcribers." The literary labors of these years were prodigious. In the persecution under Decius he was put in prison and tortured. He was released at the death of Decius but, broken in health by his suffering, he died in A.D. 253.

He was a very voluminous author. Jerome says that he wrote more than any man could read. It is related that he wrote six thousand volumes. In exegetical works, he wrote on practically the whole Bible. His main title for fame rests upon the *First Principles,* a work on systematic theology; this was written while he was young. He is said to have worked twenty-eight years upon the *Hexapla* or six-columned Bible. Six different versions of the Bible were written in parallel columns and made nearly fifty volumes. His *Against Celsus* is a noble defense of Christianity written in answer to one of the greatest skeptical philosophers of his time. He also wrote many practical works on many subjects.

ORIGEN ON HOLINESS

In about A.D. 210 he refers to the custom then practiced of praying for the newly baptized to be filled with the Holy Spirit.

Unction of Christ

In the *Seventy Homily of Ezekiel* he says:

> The unction of Christ, of holy doctrine, is the oil by which the holy man is anointed, having been instructed in the Scriptures, and taught how to be baptized; then changing a few things he [the minister] says to him, You are no longer a catechumen, now you are regenerated; such a man receives the unction of God.

Live Above Sin

He believes that we can live above sin. From *First Principles*, Book III, chapter 1, we read:

> Since in the preaching of the church there is included the doctrine respecting a just judgment of God, which, when believed to be true, incites those who hear it to live virtuously, and to shun sin by all means, inasmuch as they manifestly acknowledge that things of praise and blame are within our power.

Two Works

In Book IV, chapter 1, we read:

> As now by participating in the Son of God one is adopted as a son, and by participating in that wisdom which is in God is rendered wise, so also by participation in the Holy Spirit is a man rendered holy and spiritual.

Here two distinct and separate acts are mentioned, adoption as sons and rendered holy by the Holy Spirit—what Wesley called a "second blessing, properly so-called."

Sin No More

He mentioned the twofold mission of Jesus to save the sinner and to keep the saint above sin in his *Against Celsus*, Book III, chapter 62:

> God the Word was sent, indeed, as a physician to sinners, but as a teacher of divine mysteries to those who are already pure and who sin no more. But Celsus, unable to see this distinction—for he had not desire to be animated with a love of truth—remarks, "Why was he not sent to those who were without sin? What evil is not to have committed sin?" To which we reply, that if by those "who were without sin" he means those who sin no more, then our Saviour was sent to such, but not as a physician. While if by those "who were without sin" he means such as have never at any time sinned—for he made no distinction in his statement—we reply that it is impossible for a man thus to be without sin; for all have sinned at some time.

Pure in Heart See God

Again in answering Celsus he says (Book VII, chapter 45):

> But let us see further what the things are which he proposes to teach us, if we can comprehend them, since he [Celsus] speaks of us as being utterly wedded to the flesh; although if we live well, and in accordance with the teaching of Jesus, we hear this said of us: "Ye are not in the flesh, but in the Spirit, if the Spirit of God dwelleth in you." He says also that we look upon nothing that is pure, although our endeavor is to keep even our thoughts free from all defilement of sin, and although in prayer we say, "Create in me a clean heart, O God, and renew a right spirit within me," so that we may hold Him

with that pure heart to which alone is granted to
see Him.

Only the pure in heart can see God. As a modern writer
says, "Holiness or hell."

THE COMMENTARIES OF ORIGEN

Although Origen is the first interpreter of the Scriptures, he speaks of those who had preceded him. Many
of his comments are just and shrewd; but the tenets of the
Alexandria school, where he was, led him to many ex-
travagances. Only fragments of most of his commentaries
remain. He held that divine things were wrapped up
in mysteries, and that everything in Scripture has mys-
tical meaning in addition to that which is obvious. He
was the first great teacher who deliberately set himself
to the task of explaining the Scriptures, and for fifty
years he continued this work and treated almost the whole
Bible. His commentaries on John are the first work of
Christian exegesis which has come down to us. As it has
reached us, there are thirty-two volumes, and the first
five of these were written before A.D. 231.

HOLINESS IN ORIGEN'S COMMENTARY ON JOHN

Canaan Land

In Books 25 and 26 he shows that the crossing of the
Jordan by Joshua and the Children of Israel is symbolical
of the baptism of the Holy Ghost. Drawing from the
meaning of the word Jordan, meaning going down, consecration is pictured and the entering of Canaan points
to the land of rest that awaits all who make their consecration complete.

From Book 25:

> Let us look at the words of the Gospel now before
> us. "Jordan" means "their going down" .... What
> river will "their going down" be, to which one must
> come to be purified, a river going down, not with
> its own descent, but "theirs," namely, of men, who

but our Saviour who separates those who received their lots from Moses from those who obtain their portion through Jesus (Joshua)? His current, flowing in the descending stream, making glad, as we find in the Psalms, the city of God, not the visible Jerusalem—for it has no rivers beside it—but the blameless Church of God, built on the foundation of the Apostles and Prophets, Jesus Christ our Lord being the chief corner-stone. Under the Jordan, accordingly, we have to understand the Word of God who became flesh and tabernacled among us, Jesus who gives us as our inheritance the humanity which He assumed, for that is the head corner-stone, which being taken up into the deity of the Son of God, is washed by being so assumed, and then receives into itself the pure and guileless dove of the Spirit, bound to it and no longer able to fly away from it. For "Upon whomsoever," we read, "thou shalt see the Spirit descending and abiding upon Him, the same is He that baptizeth with the Holy Spirit." Hence, he who receives the Spirit abiding on Jesus himself is able to baptize those who come to him in that abiding Spirit.

CHAPTER EIGHT

Cyprian, the Bishop of Carthage

CYPRIAN AND HIS WORKS

THASIUS CYPRIAN was born about A.D. 200. We know very little of his early life. He was wealthy and highly educated; by profession he was an orator and teacher of rhetoric. He was converted in middle life in A.D. 246. He was the owner of some of the finest pleasure-grounds in Carthage, which he sold after his conversion for the benefit of the poor. His friends rebought it and gave it to him. His ordination and elevation to the office of a bishop rapidly followed his conversion. Because of his position and outstanding character he was made a bishop in A.D. 248, and one of the greatest of his time. He was a pupil of Tertullian and followed many of his ideas, but differed on the position that the Church held and on a few other questions.

His time as a bishop was marked by many struggles: first against the persecution of Decius, during which he went into retirement for fourteen months; then against the disorders of the Church, principally about discipline. Many had lapsed back into idolatry during persecution, and when peace was restored they asked to be restored to communion again. Some in the Church contended that the lapsed should be restored on the easiest terms; others were more strict and would not allow them to return at all. In some cases, after they had proved themselves for many years or were about to be martyred, they were allowed to come into the Church again. At the council of the African bishops under the presidency of Cyprian a middle and more reasonable course was taken.

The fact that he had risen to the bishopric within two years after his conversion caused a spirit of jealousy on the part of some. During the year he wrote many letters from his place of concealment to the clergy at Carthage, controlling, warning, directing, and exhorting; and in every way he maintained his episcopal superintendence in his absence, in all matters relative to the welfare of the church at Carthage. The first thirty-nine of his epistles, except the one to Donatus, were written during his retirement. Felicissimus opposed his method. Both the bishops at Carthage and Rome began to oppose him. Novatius went to Rome, and schisms arose which caused Cyprian much trouble.

After some time persecutions began again against the Christians from the state, and Cyprian did not escape. He was banished by Valerian and beheaded in A.D. 258.

Cyprian's theory of the Church was that it is one visible body, presided over by bishops, each of which is free and independent in his own sphere, and yet acts in council with the others for the good of the whole. His ideals for the Church had to be destroyed by decreedalism before the papacy could exist.

The Christian Lapsi

This term was used for those apostates from Christianity who lapsed back into idolatry. Decius published an edict against the Christians in A.D. 250. The procedure was as follows: The magistrates were bidden to assemble the Christians together and command them to sacrifice. Those who consented were subjected to no further annoyance and were given certificates indicating the same. The certificates were called libelli. Recent excavation has brought to light several of these. One from Egypt reads: "To the superintendents of offerings and sacrifices at the city. From Aurelius. It has been my custom to make sacrifices and pour libations to the gods and now I have in your presence in accordance with your commands poured libations and sacrifice and tasted the offerings together with my son Aurelius Dioscuros and my daughter Aurelia Lais. I therefore request you to certify my statement. The first year of the Emperor Caesar Gaius, Messius Quintus Trajanus Decius."

If this was from a Christian who had lapsed back into idolatry, how little did he think that his record would be read almost two thousand years later! How careful we should be about our records!

Cyprian on Holiness

From the writings of Cyprian and others it seems that it was the common practice to pray for the new converts that they might be filled with the Spirit. They were following up the example of Peter and John, who went down to Samaria and found disciples there who had been baptized, yet had not the Holy Ghost. They prayed for and laid their hands upon them, that the newly converted ones might receive the Holy Ghost (see Acts 8:15-17).

Heavenly Contest

Cyprian recognized that some of the martyrs were filled with the Holy Spirit. We read from his Epistle 7, *To the Martyrs,* of their devotion:

> The multitude of those present saw with admiration the heavenly contest—the spiritual contest, the battle of Christ—saw that His servants stood with free voice, unyielding mind—bare indeed of weapons of the world, but believing and armed with the weapons of faith. The tortured stood more brave than the torturers; the limbs were beaten and torn, overcame the hooks that bent and tore them. The scourge repeated with all rage could not conquer their invincible faith.

A few sentences later we read:

> A voice filled with the Holy Spirit broke from the martyr's mouth which the most blessed Mappalicus

said to the proconsul in the midst of his torments, "Ye shall see a contest tomorrow."

Laying on Hands

Cyprian recognized that it took more than the mere praying for and anointing with oil and laying hands upon to get the Holy Ghost. And some might pretend to help others get the Holy Ghost who did not have Him themselves. In Epistle 69, *To Januarius and Other Numidian Bishops,* he says:

> But how can he clean and sanctify the water who is himself unclean and in whom the Holy Spirit is not? . . . . It is necessary that he should be anointed who is baptized; so that having received the chrism, that is the anointing, he may be anointed of God, and have in him the grace of Christ. Further, it is the Eucharist whence the baptized are anointed with the oil sanctified on the altar. But he cannot sanctify the creature of oil, who has neither an altar or a church; whence also there can be no spiritual anointing among heretics since it is manifest that the oil cannot be sanctified . . . . Therefore he must be baptized and renewed who comes untrained to the church, that he may be sanctified within by those who are holy, since it is written, "Be ye holy, for I am holy, saith the Lord."

Commenting still further on baptism in Epistle 70, he says:

> And he who of his own authority grants this advantage to them, yields and consents to them, that the enemy and adversary of Christ should seem to have the power of washing, and purifying, and sanctifying a man.

Fully Sanctified

In Epistle 71, speaking of those who have been baptized outside of the church and have been stained among heretics, he says:

When they come to us and to the church which is one, ought to be baptized for the reason that it is a small matter to lay hands on them that they may receive the Holy Ghost unless they receive also the baptism of the church. For then finally they can be fully sanctified.

Lord's Seal

In Epistle 72, *To Jubaianus,* concerning the baptism of heretics, these words occur:

But if, according to a perverted faith, one can be baptized without, and obtain remission of sins, according to the same faith he could also attain the Holy Ghost; there is no need that hands should be laid upon him when he comes, that he might obtain the Holy Ghost, and be sealed.

He speaks of the Church in his day following the example of Peter and John at Samaria in these words:

Only that which was needful was performed by Peter and John; viz., that prayer should be made for them, and hands being imposed, the Holy Spirit should be invoked and poured out upon them, which now too is done among us, so that they who are baptized in the church are brought to the prelates of the church, and by our prayers and by the imposing of hands obtain the Holy Spirit, and are perfected with the Lord's seal.

Spirit for the Saved

He shows that it is the saved man who is fitted to receive the Holy Spirit. In Epistle 73:

For if anyone out of the church can become God's temple, why cannot also the Holy Spirit be poured out upon the temple? For he who has been sanctified, and his sins put away in baptism, has been spiritually reformed into a new man, has become fitted to receive the Holy Spirit.

In the same epistle we read:

For water alone is not able to cleanse away sins, and to sanctify a man, unless he have also the Holy Spirit. Wherefore it is necessary that they grant the Holy Spirit to be there, where they say baptism is; or else there is baptism where the Holy Spirit is not.

Spouse of Christ

And again:

For the church alone which, conjoined and united with Christ, spiritually bears sons; for the same apostle again says, "Christ loved the church, and gave himself for it, that he might sanctify it, cleansing it with the washing of water." If, then, she is the beloved and spouse who alone is sanctified by Christ, and alone is cleansed by His washing, it is manifest that heresy, which is not the spouse of God, nor can be cleansed nor sanctified by His washing, cannot bear sons to God.

* * * * *

But further one is not born by the imposition of hands when he received the Holy Ghost, but is baptized, that so, being already born, he may receive the Holy Spirit.

* * * * *

But as the birth of Christians is in baptism, while the generation of sanctification of baptism are with the spouse of Christ alone, who is able spiritually to conceive and bear sons to God.

From Epistle 75, we read:

And therefore, in order that, according to the divine arrangement and the evangelical truth, they may be able to obtain remission of sins, and be sanctified, and become the temples of God, they must absolutely be baptized with the baptism of the church.

Spiritual Vigor

From the *Treatise of Cyprian*, Number 10, Chapter 14, we see that he taught that we are to mortify the deeds of the flesh and live holy:

—55—

Vices and carnal sins must be trampled down, beloved brethren, and the corrupting plague of the earthly body must be trodden under foot with spiritual vigor, lest, while we are turned back again to the conversation of the old man, we be entangled in deadly snares, even as the apostle, with foresight and wholesomeness, forewarned us of this very thing, and said; "therefore, brethren, let us not live after the flesh, for if ye live after the flesh, ye shall begin to die; but if ye, through the Spirit, mortify the deeds of the flesh, we shall live. For as many as are led by the Spirit of God they are the sons of God." If we are the sons of God, if we are already beginning to be His temples, if, having received the Holy Spirit, we are living holily and spiritually, if we have raised our eyes from earth to heaven, if we have lifted our hearts, filled with God and Christ to things above and divine, let us do nothing but what is worthy of God.

CHAPTER NINE

The Church Emerging Triumphantly from Persecution

FROM the time that our Saviour hung upon the cross it was dangerous to profess Christianity. Stephen and James were killed in the early chapters of Acts. The first enmity was from Jewish hatred, and even the attacks upon St. Paul were stopped by the Roman power. Gradually this protection gave place to an enmity from Rome greater than that from the Jews. After the great fire at Rome in A.D. 64, Nero was suspected of causing it, and he sought to recover favor again by accusing the Christians of setting the city on fire. From this time on the sword, the flame, and the wild beasts were used to quench the zeal and faith of the followers of Christ. It became a crime to profess Christianity apart from any accusations against them. The persecutions were carried on with horrible brutality. Rome was soon drunk with the blood of the saints. The persecution under Domitian (A.D. 81-96) was personal, and he sought to remove any who were dangerous or obnoxious to him. His own cousin, Flavius Clemens, was executed; and Domitilla, the wife of Clemens, was banished. And on the other hand, when the grandsons of Jude, the Lord's brother, were brought before him as those who might be claimants of the throne, he dismissed them contemptuously when he found that they were only simple peasants. In all there were ten great Roman persecutions. Usually they were temporary and local; but beginning with Decius, A.D. 250, they were systematic attempts to exterminate Christianity itself.

The charges against the Christians were, first, that they rejected the gods and their images; a more serious charge was that of a want of patriotism. They refused to worship the emperor's image, and this was felt to be an unpatriotic act. They were expecting the speedy return of Christ and shrank from public offices. Lastly they were charged with immorality; their secret meetings in which they talked of love, sacrifice, blood, and body gave rise to rumors that were not seriously believed.

In spite of all the persecutions, the more they were tortured the faster they grew. Tertullian says, "We are of yesterday, and yet we have filled everything that is yours, your cities, islands, fortresses, towns, assemblies, your very camps, tribes, regiments, palace, senate, forum; we have left to you nothing but the temples."

The Church at Alexandria

Christianity is greatly indebted to the church in North Africa. One of the early Christian schools was located at Alexandria. The moral grandeur and predominance of the See of Alexandria was conspicuous in early Christian thought. Here arose Pantænus, Clement, Origen, Gregory Thaumaturgus, Dionysius, Julius Africanus, Peter of Alexandria, Alexander, Athanasius, and other characters.

GREGORY THAUMATURGUS

His surname means wonder-worker, and he was believed to be gifted with the power to work miracles. He was born about A.D. 205 at Neo-Cæsarea. He was born of heathen parents who had moderate wealth, and he lived like other Gentile boys until the death of his father; then he was placed by his brother under an accomplished teacher of rhetoric. He was a student in the celebrated law school of Berytus, but became a Christian under the teaching of Origen. He was made a bishop about A.D. 244. He shrank from the episcopal office, and those who sought to ordain him had to use stratagem and ordain him in his absence. So well did he perform his duties that it was said of him that when he entered the city as a bishop there were only seventeen Christians there and when he died there were only seventeen pagans in the city. He died about A.D. 270. His labors were divided between authorship, administration of church affairs, and evangelistic work. So great was his zeal and so exemplary his life that some of his contemporaries attributed to him marvelous powers.

GREGORY THAUMATURGUS ON HOLINESS

Perfect Image of Perfection

From his *A Declaration of Faith,* a creed on the doctrine of the Trinity, we read:

> And there is one Holy Spirit, having His subsistence from God, and being manifest by the Son, to wit to man: Image of the Son, perfect image of the Perfect; Life, the cause of the living; Holy Fount; sanctity, the Supplier, or Leader, of sanctification; in whom is manifested God the Father, who is above all, and in all, and God the Son who is through all.

Here he recognizes that the Holy Spirit is a *Perfect Image of the Perfect, the Supplier of Sanctification.*

A Personal Sanctifier

A Sectional Confession of Faith, edited in Latin by Gerardus Vossius, is attributed to him. This document shows that the Holy Spirit is a person and the One who sanctifies. In chapter four we read:

> One therefore is God the Father, one the Word, one the Spirit, the life, the sanctification of all. And neither is there another God as Father, nor is there another Son as Word of God, nor is there another Spirit as quickening and sanctifying.

Fountain of Sanctification

From chapter five we read:

> That man, consequently, belies the fountain of sanctification, the Holy Spirit, who denudes Him of

the power of sanctifying, and he will thus be pro- cluded from numbering Him with the Father and Son; he makes nought, too, of the holy ordinance of baptism, and will no more be able to acknowl- edge the holy and august Trinity. For either he must apprehend the perfect Trinity in its natural glory, or we shall be under the necessity of speak- ing no more of a Trinity . . . . We must also not number what is sanctified with the Sanctifier.

JULIUS AFRICANUS

Another great Christian scholar from the school at Alexandria, he was born in Libya, and made his home at Emmaus near Jerusalem from A.D. 195 to 240. His greatest work is a chronology from creation to A.D. 221. His other works are: *The Epistle of Aristides, Narrative of Events Happening in Persia at the Birth of Christ,* and *The Martyrdom of Symphorosa and Her Seven Sons.* He is said to be a man of unspotted character, giving evident proof of honesty and integrity.

The Story of Symphorosa and Her Seven Sons

A digest of this story will reveal the true spirit of the martyrs of the early centuries of the Church.

Adrian had built a palace and wished to dedicate it with wicked ceremonies of sacrifices to idols. The widow Sym- phorosa and her seven sons were accused of praying to God. Adrian ordered her to be seized and brought with her sons and commanded them to offer sacrifices to the idols. She replied: "My husband Getulius and his broth- er, when they were tribunes in the service, suffered dif- ferent punishments in the name of Christ, rather than consent to sacrifice to idols; like good athletes they were overcome by death . . . . They enjoy eternal life with the King eternal in the heavens."

Then Emperor Adrian said to her, "Either sacrifice along with thy sons or I will cause thee to be sacrificed to the gods." She replied, "Thy gods cannot take me in sacrifice." Again he demanded that she choose. And she replied: "Thou thinkest that my mind can be altered by some kind of terror; whereas I desire to rest with my husband."

The emperor ordered her to be led to the temple and first to be beaten, then suspended by the hair. When he could not persuade her to change, a large stone was tied to her neck and she was thrown into the river.

On another day the emperor ordered all her sons to be brought, and challenged them to sacrifice to the idols. When he saw that they yielded to none of his threats and terrors, he ordered that seven stakes be fixed around the temple of Hercules and commanded that they be stretched on their backs there. Crescens, the first, he ordered to be cut in the throat; Julian to be stabbed in the breast; Nemesius to be struck through the heart; Primitivus to be wounded in the body; Justin to be struck in the back with a sword; Stracteus to be wounded on the side; and Eugenius to be cleft in twain from the head downwards. The next day he ordered that their bodies be carried together and cast into a deep pit. And after this, persecution ceased for a year and a half, and the bodies of the holy martyrs were honored.

METHODIUS, THE LAST MARTYR OF THE EARLY PERSECUTIONS

We do not know the date of his birth, but he suffered martyrdom about the year A.D. 312, at Chalcis, Greece. Some think it was a city of the same name in Syria. He was bishop of Olympus, but afterwards moved to Tyre in Phœnecia according to Jerome. He was a contemporary with Porphyry, the heathen philosopher whom he opposed. He is known chiefly for his antagonism to Origen; yet he was greatly influenced by Origen's method of allegorical interpretation of scripture. Epiphanius calls him "a very learned man and a strenuous asserter of the truth."

The only complete work of his that has come down to us is his *Banquet of the Ten Virgins*. This is a dialogue praising the virginal life. We have parts of his treatise *On the Resurrection,* and *On Things Created,* and *On Free Will.*

METHODIUS ON HOLINESS

At the close of his dialogue, *The Banquet of the Ten Virgins,* Discourse II, chapter two, we have Thekla singing a hymn with the rest of the ten virgins, the Church, the spouse of God, pure and virgins. In the hymn are twenty-four stanzas, each followed by the same chorus.

Stanzas two, three, and four with the chorus read as follows:

> *Thekla.* 2. Fleeing from the sorrowful happiness of mortals, and having despised the luxuriant delight of life and its love, I desire to be protected under thy life-giving arms, and to behold thy beauty for ever, O blessed one.

> *Chorus.* I keep myself pure for thee, O bridegroom, and holding a lighted torch I go to meet thee.

> *Thekla.* 3. Leaving marriage and the life of mortals and my golden home for thee, O King, I have come in undefiled robes, in order that I may enter with thee within thy happy bridal chamber.

> *Chorus.* I keep myself pure for thee, O bridegroom, and holding a lighted torch I go to meet thee.

> *Thekla.* 4. Having escaped, O Blessed One, from the innumerable enchanting wiles of the serpent, and, moreover, from the flames of fire, and from the mortal destroying assaults of wild beasts, I await thee from heaven.

> *Chorus.* I keep myself pure for thee, O bridegroom, and holding a lighted torch I go to meet thee.

VICTORIANUS

We do not know much about him. He was a native of Africa but went to Rome about A.D. 200 to teach rhetoric; for he was a Latin teacher of grammar, rhetoric, and philosophy. He became a Christian in late life and was a teacher of Jerome. His *Commentaries* on some of the books of the Bible and his *Polemics* against the Arians and Manichaeans are worthy of attention, but his chief fame is as a grammarian.

VICTORIANUS ON HOLINESS

From his *Commentary on the Apocalypse*, chapter 4: 6, we read, "The burning torches of fire signify the gift of the Holy Spirit."

White Robes

From chapter 6: 9 we read: "And for a solace to their body, there were given unto each of them white robes. They received, says he, white robes, that is, the gift of the Holy Spirit."

From these comments we see that he believed in the gift of the Holy Spirit and was trying to make a spiritual application of the symbolical facts found in the Book of Revelation.

DIONYSIUS, BISHOP OF ROME

He was Greek by birth, and a good representative of the spirit and orthodoxy of the Greek fathers. Even before he became the Bishop of Rome he must have been one of the most distinguished members of the church there, for his namesake at Alexandria addresses two letters to him. He was the Bishop of Rome from A.D. 259 to 269. At this time the churches were beginning to look to Rome as superior. Dionysius of Rome reviewed the teachings of Dionysius of Alexandria on the Trinity, and a letter was sent to the Egyptian churches. He did much to reorganize the Church after the severe persecution through which it had come.

A fragment of one of his epistles of treatise, *Against the Sabellians*, exists today.

DIONYSIUS OF ROME ON HOLINESS

From his *Against the Sabellians* we quote where he is arguing against the creation of the Son of God, these words:

> But why should I discourse at greater length to you about these matters, since ye are men filled with the Spirit, and especially understand what absurd results follow from the opinion which asserts that the Son was made?

CHAPTER TEN

The First Church Manuals and Liturgies

THE "DIDACHE," OR TEACHING OF THE TWELVE APOSTLES

The Oldest Church Manual in Existence. The date of its composition is uncertain, but it is probably not later than A.D. 150; some scholars are of the opinion that it is from the first century. We know absolutely nothing about the author. A few Hebrewisms occur, and this may indicate that it was written by a Jewish Christian. The genuineness of the document is universally admitted. An old manuscript of this document was found by Archbishop Bryennios in a volume containing the writings of other fathers in 1873.

The Contents of the "Didache"

It begins with a description of the Two Ways, of Life and Death. This was used for the instruction of the converts. Then there follows a series of instructions on church rites and customs. Directions are given in chapter seven on how to baptize, in running water if possible; if not, in still water or by affusion, in either cold or warm water. More emphasis is placed upon the spiritual preparation for baptism than upon the mode. Fasting upon Wednesdays and Fridays is enjoined, and the saying of the Lord's Prayer three times a day. A form for the consecration of the cup and bread is given for the Lord's Supper. The prophets or preachers are not to be bound by formal prayers. Different orders are recognized in the ministry; a distinction is recognized between the fixed ministry and the prophet.

Flee Every Evil

Chapter three begins:

> My child, flee every evil thing, and from everything like it. Be not prone to anger, for anger leadeth to murder; nor jealous, nor contentious, nor passionate, for of all these murders are begotten. My child, become not lustful, for lust leadeth to fornication; nor foul-mouthed, nor lofty-eyed, for of all these adulteries are begotten. My child, become not an omen-watcher, since it leadeth unto idolatry; nor an astrologer, nor a purifier, nor be willing to look on these things, for of all these things idolatry is begotten. My child, become not a liar, since lying leadeth to theft; nor avaricious, nor vainglorious, for of all these thefts are begotten. My child, become not a murmurer, since it leadeth to blasphemy; nor presumptuous, nor evil-minded, for of all these things blasphemies are begotten. But be meek, for the meek shall inherit the earth. Become long-suffering, and pitiful, and guileless, and gentle and good, and tremble continually at the words which thou hast heard.

They contended for a high spiritual life.

Sanctified True Church

From the *Didache* we see that the Early Church considered the sanctified ones as composing the true Church. From chapter ten we read:

> Remember, Lord, Thy Church, to deliver it from every evil, and to make it perfect in Thy love, and gather it from the four winds, it, the sanctified into Thy Kingdom, which Thou hast prepared for it, for Thine is the power and glory forever. Let grace come and let this world pass away. Hosanna to the Son of David! Whoever is holy, let him come; whoever is not, let him repent. Maranatha. Amen.

The Early Church prayed to be made perfect in love and for deliverance from all evil, testified that the sanctified ones were the true Church of God, and shouted, "Glory!" "Hosanna!" "Amen." Are you living up to their standard?

APOSTOLIC CONSTITUTIONS AND CANONS

The *Constitutions* are a collection of ecclesiastical ordinances, in eight books. The claim was made for them that they were the work of the apostles and written down by St. Clement. But this is not correct. The best scholars on church history are now about agreed that the *Apostolic Constitutions* are a compilation from material derived from sources differing in age. The first six of the books are the oldest part. The *Didache* seems to be the basis of the seventh book. And the eighth book is the latest part composed. It is generally admitted that entire work is not later than the fourth century, and the first six books can hardly be later than the second or third century. Early writers are inclined to assign parts of it to the days of the apostles if not to the apostles themselves. There is every indication that it was compiled of earlier and long-used sources. Recent research has awakened new interest in the *Apostolic Constitutions* by the discovery of an old manuscript of it in Constantinople.

The purpose of this work was to present a manual of instruction, worship, polity, and usage.

The Apostolic Canons, so-called, are found in the last part of the eighth book of the Constitutions. There are eighty-five of them. They were probably composed in Syria.

THE APOSTOLIC CONSTITUTIONS ON HOLINESS

Worldliness Condemned

From Book I, Section 2. Concerning Adornment and the Sin that arises therefrom. Worldliness is condemned. "Thou shalt not put a gold ring upon thy finger," is one sentence found. But beauty of heart is encouraged. We read, "For thou art not to please man, so as to commit sin; but God, so as to attain holiness of life, and be a partaker of eternal rest."

Anointed with Oil

In Book III, Section 2, the question of Holy Baptism is discussed, and the bishop is required to anoint with oil the one who has been baptized. The meaning of this is explained in these words, "This baptism is given, therefore, into the death of Christ; the water instead of the burial, and the oil instead of the Holy Ghost."

From Book V, Section 1, we read concerning martyrs: "For he that is condemned for the name of the Lord Jesus Christ is an holy martyr, a receptacle of the Holy Spirit."

In Book VII, Section 3, Chapter 39, the catechumens are instructed.

His Creation

To thank God, for His creation, for sending Christ His only begotten Son, that He might save man by blotting out his transgressions, and that He might remit ungodliness, and might purify him from all filthiness of flesh and spirit, and sanctify man according to the good pleasure of His kindness, that He might inspire him with a knowledge of His will, and enlighten the eyes of his heart to consider His wonderful works, and make known unto him the ways of righteousness, that he might hate every way of iniquity, and walk in the way of truth.

Consecration of Deaconesses

From Book VIII, Section 3, chapter 20, we read from the prayer for the ordination of a deaconess:

Do Thou now also look down upon this Thy servant, who is to be ordained to the office of a deaconess, and grant her Thy Holy Spirit, and cleanse her from all filthiness of the flesh and spirit that she may worthily discharge the work which is committed to her.

Consecration of Readers

From the same book, and chapter 22, from the prayer for the consecration of the readers we read:

> Do Thou also now look down upon Thy servant, who is to be intrusted with the reading of Thy Holy Scriptures to Thy people, and give him Thy Holy Spirit, the prophetic Spirit. Thou who didst instruct Esdras Thy servant to read the law to Thy people, do Thou also at our prayers instruct Thy servant, and grant that he may without blame perfect the work committed to him, and thereby be declared worthy of a higher degree, through Christ, with whom glory and worship be to Thee and the Holy Ghost forever. Amen.

Great emphasis was placed upon all the officers of the church having the Holy Ghost.

It was spiritual worthiness that was considered, for even a bishop could be consecrated who was physically maimed yet spiritually qualified. From *The Apostolic Canons No.* 77 we read:

> If any one be maimed in the eye or lame in the leg, but is worthy of episcopal dignity, let him be made a bishop; for it is not a blemish of the body that can defile him, but the pollution of the soul.

The Early Liturgies

We who are accustomed to extemporaneous prayer and freedom of church ritual do not recognize the great influence that the liturgies have held on the Church at different periods of church history.

The liturgy was a form of public worship, especially for the celebration of the Lord's Supper. From the days of the apostles there has been a form for the observance of the Eucharist. The references to the liturgy in the first three centuries are not so numerous; but comparing them with those after the Nicaean Council, there must have been a great similarity between them. Various liturgies have come down to us from the early centuries but of their age, authorship, and genuineness we are not certain. The most interesting of these are the liturgies of St. Mark, St. James, St. Clement, St. Chrysostom, and that of St. Basil. The ancient liturgies are divided into the Liturgy of Jerusalem, used in the East; the Alexandrian, used in Egypt; the Roman; and the Persian; the Clementine also may be mentioned, but it seems that it never was used as a form for public worship. It is found in the eighth book of the *Apostolic Constitutions.*

The liturgies were usually divided into two parts: the parts before and after the words, "Lift we up our hearts."

HOLINESS IN THE EARLY LITURGIES

Prayers for Perfection

From the *Divine Liturgy of St. James,* Part I, Division 3. At the beginning of the Prayer of Incense, these words occur:

> Accept from us, Thy unprofitable servants, this incense as an odour of a sweet smell, and make fragrant the evil odour of our soul and body, and purify us with the sanctifying power of Thy all-holy Spirit.

From Division 4:

> Fulfill to each what is profitable; lead all to perfection and make us perfectly worthy of Thy sanctification.

From Division 13: The Prayer of the Deacon, these words occur:

> Let us entreat from the Lord, that we may pass the whole day, perfect, holy, peaceful, and without sin.
>
> God and Sovereign of all, make us, who are unworthy, worthy of this hour, lover of mankind; that being free from all deceit, and all hypocrisy, we may be united with one another by the bond of peace and love being confirmed by the sanctification of Thy divine knowledge.

From Division 29, we read:

O Holy art Thou, King of eternity, and Lord and giver of all holiness.

From *The Divine Liturgy of St. Mark*, Division 4, we read:

O Lord, deliver us. Purify our lives and cleanse our hearts from all pollution and from all wickedness, that with pure hearts and consciences we may offer to Thee this incense.

Cherubic Hymns

From Division 10: After the singing of the cherubic hymn, pray thus:

O holy, highest, awe-inspiring God, who dwellest among saints, sanctify us, and deem us worthy of Thy reverent priesthood. Bring us to Thy precious altar with a good conscience, and cleanse our hearts from pollution. Drive away from us all unholy thoughts and sanctify our souls and minds.

From Division 17, we read:

Send down from Thy holy heaven, from the mansion which Thou hast prepared, and from Thy faithful bosom, the Paraclete himself, holy, powerful, and life-giving, the Spirit of truth, who spoke in the law, the apostles, and prophets; who is everywhere present, filling all things, freely working sanctification in whom He will.

CHAPTER ELEVEN

Interesting Early Christian Literature

TESTAMENT OF THE TWELVE PATRIARCHS

THIS curious fragment of antiquity deserves a few words of study. It is important to us because of its high ethical teachings. It was used freely in the early centuries, but soon afterward it disappeared and was unmentioned until a manuscript of it was found in the thirteenth century. There is a verbal correspondence between it and some of the New Testament. There are allusions to several books of the New Testament.

The work professes to be the utterances of the dying patriarchs, the twelve sons of Jacob. It gives the lives of each, embodying some events not found in the Old Testament, and stresses their virtues for the guidance of those who follow them. The book appears in the form of an Apocalypse, picturing the future of their descendants doing wickedly and foretelling the troubles befalling the Jewish race. Also, it shows that God will put an end to their trouble by the coming of the Messiah. The author was looking for a speedy coming of Christ and believed in the resurrection of the body.

The author was doubtless a Jew who had been converted to Christianity. The date of its composition cannot be placed very far in the second century, for it is quoted by both Tertullian and Origen. From internal evidences it appears that it could not have been written later than the revolt of Bar-Cochaba in A.D. 135. It was written between A.D. 109 and 135.

THE TESTAMENT OF THE TWELVE PATRIARCHS ON HOLINESS

Virtue, righteousness, and holiness are encouraged throughout in the twelve divisions of the book. The spirit of the Sermon on the Mount appears all through it. We will offer two quotations.

An Open Heaven

From Part III, The Testament of Levi concerning the priesthood and arrogance, Div. 18:

> The heavens shall be opened, and from the temple of glory shall the sanctification rest upon Him with the Father's voice, as from Abraham the father of Isaac. And the glory of the Most High shall be uttered over Him, and the Spirit of understanding and of sanctification shall rest upon Him in the water. He shall give the majesty of the Lord to His sons in truth for evermore; and there shall none succeed Him for all generations, even for ever. And in His priesthood shall all sin come to an end, and the lawless shall rest from evil, and the just shall rest in Him. And He shall open the gates of Paradise, and shall remove the threatening sword against Adam; and He shall give to His saints to eat from the tree of life; and the spirit of holiness shall be upon them.

He shows that during the sanctified priesthood of Christ all sin shall be put away and the spirit of holiness shall be upon His saints.

From Part IV, The Testament of Judah concerning fortitude, Div. 24, in speaking about the ministry of Christ he says:

> And the heavens shall be opened above Him, to show forth the blessings of the Spirit from the Holy Father; and He shall show forth a spirit of grace upon you, and ye shall be unto Him sons in truth, and ye shall walk in His commandments, the first and the last.

PSEUDO-CLEMENTINE LITERATURE

The name Pseudo-Clementine Literature, or the Clementina, is applied to a series of writings closely resembling one another and claiming to have been the writings of Clement of Rome. However, the claim is probably false. These works are: (1) the Recognitions, consisting of ten books with many chapters each; (2) the Homilies, twenty in number; (3) the Epitome. Also a few others have been mentioned as the two Epistles on Virginity. They all belong to a class of fictitious literature for a purpose and were written by Jewish Christians.

The Recognitions of Clement

This is a kind of theological romance. The author does not seem to present the facts for the truth, but chooses the disciples of Christ and their friends as the principal characters, and from their discourses he weaves a story containing most of the important beliefs of the Church therein. The date and authorship have been keenly discussed, but with no uniformity of opinion. The first, second, third, and even the fourth centuries have been designated as the time of its composition. But the fact that it is quoted by Origen proves that it could not have been written any later than A.D. 231. There is scarcely another writing which is of so great importance for the history of Christianity in its early stages as this work.

The Story Given in the Recognition of Clement

The Clement of the Recognition is the chief character of the story. The first book begins by saying, "I Clement, born in the city of Rome, was from my earliest age a lover of chastity; while the bend of my mind held me bound by the chains of anxiety and sorrow." As the waves of anxiety arose, he began to seek the truth from the philosophers. As he traveled about he was more and more dissatisfied with the schools of philosophy until he finally heard of Christ and was converted by the preaching of Barnabas at Rome. He later went to Cæsarea, and was introduced to Peter, who cordially received him. He became an attendant of Peter and was instructed by him.

At this time Peter was engaged in discussion with Simon Magus in order to refute his errors. This discussion continues with many chapters on almost all the major questions of Christianity and enters into many points of Jewish history. It becomes a regular theology on Christian doctrine.

In the third book, twelve were baptized as Christians; and among them were Clement and Niceta and Aquila, who afterwards proved to be his brothers. After much discussion and instruction on Christian doctrine and usages as they traveled about, it was decided that the twelve should divide into bands for a short time. This occurs in Book 7. Clement rejoiced that he was to stay with Peter and showed great affection for him. Peter inquired about his family history; and Clement said that he came from a noble stock of the Caesars. His father was named Faustinianus, and his mother's name was Matihildia; and twin brothers were born before him, named Faustinus and Faustus. He had learned from his father that, when he was five years old, his mother had a dream that if she did not leave the city for ten years she and her children should perish by a miserable death. Then his father put his mother aboard a ship with the twins and a servant with money to go to Athens and educate the boys there. After a season he sent to Athens to find out about her; but she was not found. After sending several times, he left Clement with guardians and went to search for his wife and the children; he had not been heard of again for more than twenty years.

After this, Peter went to an island called Aradus, and while here he found a poor woman asking alms. He inquired of her why she was in this miserable plight. She told him how she was born of noble parents, and was the wife of a good man to whom were born twins and afterwards another son. Then her husband's brother tried to entice her into sin; and, to avoid this sin and bringing trouble between the brothers, she told her husband that she had had a vision indicating that she and her two sons would die a violent death unless she fled from the city for ten years. Her husband, hearing it, sent her to Athens and while she was on the way a great storm arose and they were shipwrecked, but she escaped to the shore. The next morning when it was light she tried to find her sons, but could not, and supposed they were drowned. An old woman gave her refuge with her in a hut, and they had lived together until the woman was afflicted, and now she was trying to support both by begging. At this Peter was astonished and inquired of her from what country she came; she feigned one thing after another, and said she was an Ephesian. Then Peter said, "Alas, I thought that some joy had come to you today; for I had suspicioned that you were a certain woman that I just recently heard about."

Clement had come up while they were talking, and Peter had bidden him to return to the ship before him. When the woman would hear more about this woman, Peter told her about the Roman citizen who had sent away his wife to Athens, and told her that the young man whom he had sent on to the ship was the son. Then she cried out, "He is my son." Peter inquired what his name was and she said Clement. And Peter said, "It is he."

Then the woman cried for Peter to lead her to the ship at once, but fainted. He lifted her up and she revived, and he took her by the hand and led her to the ship. Clement came out and she uttered a loud scream and began to embrace him. He would push her aside in astonishment, but Peter said, "Cease, what mean you, Clement? Do not push away your mother." After this happy meeting, a great multitude assembled to see what was happening. When they would depart, the woman said, "Is it right for me to depart and leave the old, sick woman who has befriended me and shared her hut?" Then Peter said in the midst of the crowd that he was a preacher of right-eousness, and they went over, and he said, "In the name of Jesus Christ, let the woman arise." Then she was healed and raised from her bed; they gave her money and departed. Clement's mother lodged with Peter's wife on the journey. She inquired of Clement about her husband, and was told that he had gone in search of her and had not been heard of since.

After this, they came to Laodicea, where Niceta and Aquila were. Peter, seeing it was a good city, decided to stay there for ten days. When Niceta and Aquila inquired who the unknown woman was, Clement told them it was his mother, whom God had given back to him.

Then Peter related the story to them of the woman. When he was telling about her seeking and crying out for her sons, Faustinus and Faustus, when she was shipwrecked, Niceta and Aquila cried out, "Are these things so, or are we in a dream?" Peter said, "Unless we are mad men, they are so." Then they said, "We are Faustinus and Faustus." And they would go at once and embrace their mother, who was sleeping. But Peter asked that they let him prepare her mind for the surprise.

When she had risen, Peter went to her and spoke to her about the true religion, and she said she was ready to give up her old idolatry, and was ready to be baptized. And as she was speaking of her sons, they could scarcely refrain themselves, so rushed upon her and began to kiss her. She said, "What meaneth this?" Peter told her not to be disturbed, for they were her sons, Faustinus and Faustus.

Then Niceta told his mother how on the night that they were shipwrecked they were captured by pirates and sold to a very honorable woman, named Justa, and that she had had them educated in the Greek literature and philosophy. And that when they had grown up, they had been with Simon Magus and had heard Peter's discussions with him, and had become Christians. Soon she recognized her sons, and a little later she was baptized.

Then in Book 8: The next morning after, Peter and the twin brothers went out to the sea to bathe, and after that they retired to a secret place to pray. But as they prayed, a certain old man, a workman, as he appeared from his clothing, approached them to see what they were doing, and asked to converse with them. Many discussions in many chapters, on the Christian religion, follow. Almost three books are given to these discussions, and the old man is not convinced of the truth of Christianity until finally he tells of his sad fate: how his wife had fallen in love with a slave of the house, and had told him of a vision to get away from him with her twin sons, and that he had gone out to seek her, but in vain.

Peter asked him how he knew that his wife had deceived him; he then told him that his brother had said that she had first tried to get him to take her, and when he would not she told him that she had had a vision about a violent death that awaited her and her sons if she did not leave the city, that she might run away with the man with whom she had fallen in love. Then Peter asked him if he would believe and turn to Christianity if he would restore to him his chaste and true wife, with his three sons.

The old man said as it was impossible for him to do so, so it was impossible that it should take place. Then Peter pointed out his sons to him and named them. When the old man heard their names, he fainted away, and the sons came and lifted him up. At this time, the wife of the old man, having found out someway that her husband had been found, rushed up and cried out, "Where is my husband, my lord Faustinianus, who has been so long afflicted, and searching from city to city for me?" And the old man ran up and embraced her. Then Peter requested the crowd to disperse, and they returned home with him.

After a season together, the old man was instructed by Peter and his family, and finally believed and was baptized. Simon Magus tried to keep the old man from the way of truth, but Peter refuted his discussion, and all ended happily.

The Recognitions of Clement on Holiness

Filled with Spirit

From Book II, chapter 21, the following is given as the words of Peter:

> Then going to God chaste and clean, we shall be filled with the Holy Spirit.

In speaking of baptism in Book III, chapter 67, these words occur:

> He being first anointed with oil sanctified with prayer, that so at length, being consecrated by these things, he may attain a perception of holy things.

The Clementine Homilies on Holiness

All the existing early fragments of Christian sermons for the first three centuries are in the form of homilies. In the Clementine collection there are twenty of these.

In Homily II, chapter 42, "The Right Notions of God Essential to Holiness," we find these words:

> But I do not think, my dear Clement, that any one who possesses even so little love to God and ingenuousness, will be able to take in, or even hear, the things that are spoken to him. For how is it that he can have a monarchic soul, and be holy, who supposes that there are many gods and not one only?

CHAPTER TWELVE

The Closing of the Ante-Nicene Period

THE first three centuries of the history of the Christian Church was a time of struggle for existence. All the powers of a superstitious paganism and the prejudice of Judaism were battling against it. They were also laying the foundation for the future progress of Christianity. The chief early writings were defensive, and they had little time or occasion to formulate doctrine. As error began to creep in, it became necessary definitely to state the creeds. The deity of Christ was the first distinctive doctrine of Christianity to be stated. The Council of Nicæa was called in A.D. 325 to settle the Arian controversy. The trouble began at Alexandria. Arius, trying to safeguard the unity of God, had denied that Christ was divine and equal to the Father. Alexander, his bishop, opposed him, but soon died of old age, and Athanasius took up the struggle; and Constantine, the emperor, called a council of all the Church to settle this difficulty. More than three hundred bishops, some coming from as far as India, appeared at Nicæa, and Arius was condemned. With the nominal conversion of Constantine, the persecutions of the Christians stopped.

The opening of the council is described by Eusebius as follows:

> After all the bishops had entered the central building at the royal palace, on the sides of which were many seats prepared, each took his place with becoming modesty, and silently awaited the Emperor. The court officers entered one after another, though only such as professed faith in Christ. The moment the approach of the Emperor was announced by a given signal, they all arose from their seats, and the Emperor appeared like an heavenly messenger of God, covered with gold and gems, a

glorious presence, very tall and slender, full of beauty, strength and majesty. With the external adornment he united the spiritual ornament of the fear of God, modesty, and humility, which could be seen on his downcast eyes, his blushing face, the motion of his body, and his walk. When he reached the golden throne prepared for him, he stopped, and sat down as all the bishops gave him the sign. And after him, all resumed their seats.

What a great contrast between this scene and the Church in the days of great persecutions under the Roman emperors! Soon the primitive purity was displaced by worldliness, false teaching, and corruption; then follow the papal system and the Dark Ages. Almost all holiness and righteousness was crowded out until the days of the Protestant Reformation. Only here and there do we see a gleam of light shining out of the night of the Dark Ages.

There was a little controversy among the early writers about which books should form the canon of the New Testament; but shortly after the Nicæan Council, we find lists of all the books that we now acknowledge as the New Testament, and no others. Pappus has a low estimate on how the authentic books were found. He says: "Having promiscuously put all the books that were referred to the council for determination under the communion table, they besought the Lord that the inspired ones might get upon the table and the spurious ones under it, and that it happened accordingly." But this is only a legend. The Holy Spirit helped the early Christians to keep the inspired scriptures separate from the spurious ones.

The Apocryphal New Testament

There are more than twenty of these books. They are written in a style very similar to that of the canonical books of the New Testament, but their character is far inferior to the inspired ones. They contain some truth, and many unbelievable legends. Dr. Talmage says of them: "We are not permitted to think that the shadows of Calvary darkened His pathway as a youth, and the Apocryphal Books of the New Testament show a great deal of the earthly life of Christ not to be found in the Evangelists." Some of these books were probably written as forgeries, and others with an intention of being placed with the books of the Bible. They were all written during these early days, but at different times.

We will notice briefly a few of them:

The Gospel of Mary, The Protevangelion, I and II Infancy contain many stories about the birth and early life of Mary and Jesus. In the first two, Mary is given a supernatural birth similar to that of Christ. In the books on the Infancy, many miracles are attributed to Jesus as a Child, such as stretching out a board so it would be as long as another in the carpenter shop at Nazareth, making clay birds to fly away, the taking up of spilled water in His mantle after the pitcher had fallen and broken, and similar ones. These are absurd and unbelievable.

In *Christ and Abgarus,* the King of Edessa sends a letter to Jesus to come and heal him, and Jesus answers that He must go up and fulfill His mission, and that He will send one of His disciples to cure him.

The epistles of Clement, Barnabas, and Hermas have received separate treatment; and the letters of Herod and Pilate are interesting, but doubtless fictitious.

HOLINESS IN THE APOCRYPHAL NEW TESTAMENT

Much is said about the coming of the Holy Spirit upon Mary and Jesus in the first of these books, and the idea of purity, holiness, and sanctification is frequently mentioned in a number of the apocryphal books. The most important of these are treated in the previously mentioned books.

The Syrian Documents

Most of the early Christian documents are written in Greek or Latin, but some fifteen have reached us in the

Syrian language. Most of these relate Christian history and life; several stories of Christian martyrs occur. These are heroic and inspiring. Examples of Christian piety, courage, righteousness, and holy living are of frequent occurrence.

The First Harmony of the Gospels

The Diatessaron of Tatian is the first attempt at producing the four Gospels as one story; about two-thirds of the verses of the Gospels are used. Tatian says that he was a Syrian and a convert of Justin Martyr. He was born about A.D. 110 and perhaps saw Justin martyred in A.D. 166. His harmony was greatly appreciated in the early centuries, and manuscripts of it occur in many languages. He later became a Gnostic, and was regarded as a heretic.

Pseudo Gospels, Epistles, and Apocalypses

Recent research has brought to light many of these from the early days of Christianity; many of them are just fragments. We may mention from these *The Gospel of Peter, The Revelation of Peter, The Vision of Paul, The Apocalypse of Sedrech, The Testament of Abraham, The Acts of Zanthippe, and the Narration of Zosimus.*

Near the beginning of *The Revelation of Peter* we find these words: "And the God will come unto my faithful ones who hunger and thirst and are afflicted and purify their souls in this life; and He will judge the sons of the lawless." After this the writer says that the Lord told them to go into the mountain and pray. Then he describes a very vivid vision of paradise which he sees, and this is followed by a vision of hell.

OTHER ANCIENT FRAGMENTS

Sermons

The oldest known sermon outside of those recorded in the Bible was discovered by Bryennios in the Jerusalem monastery and published in 1875. It is from an unknown

Greek or Latin author from about the middle of the second century. It is interesting to note that it begins by addressing the hearers as "Brothers and Sisters."

Another early Christian fragment contains what seems to be a paragraph from a sermon on "The Spirit of Prophecy." It reads as follows:

> Man being filled with the Holy Ghost speaks as the Lord wills; the spirit of the divine nature will thus be manifest. For the spirit of prophecy is the essence of the prophet order which is the body of the flesh of Jesus Christ, which was mingled with human nature through Mary.

From another old sermon, speaking of Christ, we read:

> He is the Light; therefore He is the Sun of our souls. He is the Life; therefore we live in Him. He is Holiness; therefore He is the slayer of sin.

Prayers

A number of other interesting old sermons from the first centuries have been found. Also a number of fragments of old Christian prayers have been brought to light recently.

Hymns

Several very ancient Christian hymns have been discovered, but none more interesting than a collection known as the *Odes and Psalms of Solomon*. Dr. J. Rendel Harris, of Cambridge, found it in a Syriac manuscript of sixty-four leaves, and published it in 1909. Scholars regard it as the work of a Jewish Christian of the first century. It contains more than a thousand verses.

From Ode 15 we quote these words:

> Behold! the Lord is our mirror; open the eyes and see them in Him; and learn the manner of your face; and tell forth praises to His Spirit; and wipe off the filth from your face; and love His holiness, and clothe yourselves therewith; and be without stain at all times before Him. Hallelujah!

CHAPTER THIRTEEN

Eusebius, the Father of Church History

OUR study of the literature of the Early Church would not be complete without noticing the *Ecclesiastical History* by Eusebius. A few attempts at chronicling sketches of church history had been made before the days of Eusebius, but he is the first to give us a complete history of the Church to his time. All later church historians are indebted to him. The author was born in Palestine about A.D. 260. He took the surname of his teacher, Pamphilus of Caesarea, whose great library furnished him much of the extensive historical sources Eusebius used later. At the martyrdom of his teacher, Eusebius fled and was imprisoned in Egypt. In 313 he became the bishop of Caesarea. At the Council of Nicæa he made the opening address, and he led the moderate party. He stood in high favor with Constantine the Emperor, who declared him fit to be the bishop of almost the entire world. He received many letters from the Emperor and was frequently in his palace and entertained at his table.

Constantine also committed to Eusebius, since he was skilled in Biblical knowledge, the care and superintendency of transcribing the fifty copies of the Scriptures that the Emperor wished to place in the churches that he was building at Constantinople. He died at Caesarea about A.D. 340. He was the most learned of the Church Fathers after Origen, but was without his genius. His chief works are: *Chronocum*, a history of the world in his day; *The Praeparation Evangelica*, extracts from the heathen authors fitting to prepare the way for Christianity; *Demonstration Evangelica*, arguments to convince the Jews of the truths of Christianity; and his *Ecclesiastical History*, relating the principal occurrences in church history to 324—this is his greatest work and is in ten books.

EUSEBIUS ON HOLINESS
Prayer for Holy Ghost

He frequently makes mention of what seemed to be the universal custom of the Early Church when a person was baptized, for the bishop to lay hands upon the persons baptized and pray that they might be filled with the Holy Ghost. A candidate for baptism must be fully saved without question before he was a candidate for the baptism of the Holy Ghost or the experience of holiness. Eusebius gives a narration which he contends is true history about the Apostle John, in which the filling of the Spirit through the laying on of hands is called "a perfect safeguard in the seal of the Lord." This occurs in Book 3, chapter 23, and the narration briefly stated is as follows:

After John returned from the Isle of Patmos to Ephesus, he went about the neighboring regions to appoint bishops to new churches and appoint to the ministry those whom the Holy Ghost should point out. Seeing a youth of fine stature, grace, and an ardent mind, he turned to a bishop he had appointed and said, "Him I commend unto you with all earnestness, in the presence of the Church of Christ." John returned to Ephesus; and the presbyter, taking the youth home, educated, restrained, and cherished him, and at length baptized him. But, thinking he was now committed to "a perfect safeguard in the seal of the Lord," he relaxed his former care and vigilance over the youth. Then certain idle, dissolute fellows familiar with all kinds of wickedness attached themselves to him; at first by expensive entertainment, then by going out at night to plunder and taking him along. They encouraged him until gradually he became accustomed to their ways, and "like an unbridled steed that had struck out of the right way, biting the curb, he rushes with so much the greater impetuosity towards the precipice." At length he renounced salvation and became the captain of a band of robbers, surpassing them all in violence, blood, and cruelty.

John and the Robber

After a time John demanded the young man; and the old bishop said, "He is dead." John asked how. "He is dead to God," said the old bishop. "He has turned out wicked and abandoned, and at last a robber; instead of the church, he has beset the mountain with a band like himself." When the apostle heard this he tore his garments, asked for a horse and a guide, then rode out to the country and was taken prisoner by the robbers' guard. But he said, "Lead me to your captain." When the robber recognized John, he was overcome with shame, and turned to flee. But the apostle, pursuing him, cried out, "Why dost thou flee, my son, from me, thy father? Fear not; thou still hast hope of life. I will intercede with Christ for thee." Hearing this, the robber stopped with downcast looks, threw away his arms; then trembling and weeping bitterly, he came up and embraced John. The apostle pledged him that he had found pardon for his sins at the hand of Christ, praying, on bended knee, and kissing his right hand as cleansed from all iniquity. The apostle then led him back to the Church, and did not leave him until he was fully restored to salvation.

Irregular Baptisms

In Book 6, chapter 43, Eusebius tells how Novatius was baptized while sick, but was not prayed for that he might receive the Holy Ghost. On this account the bishop is condemned.

The question soon arose about what should be done with those who wished to return after they had fallen into heresy, who had previously been prayed for with the laying on of hands that they might be filled with the Holy Ghost. In Book 7, chapter 2, we read:

> Dionysius wrote the first of his epistles on baptism, as there was no little controversy, whether those turning from any heresy whatever, should be purified by baptism; as the ancient practice pre-

vailed with regard to such, that they should only have imposition of hands with prayer.

Rule of Faith

In chapter 7 of the same book he adds that it was the rule and form received from our father, the blessed Herecles, when one made public confession after he had returned from those who taught strange doctrines and come from the heresies, that they be received back without baptism, even though they had been expelled from the Church; for he says, "they had already received the Holy Spirit."

Living Holy Common Practice

Eusebius mentions a number of incidents that show that living holy and being filled with the Spirit was the common practice of the Christians in the early centuries. In Book 3, chapter 31, we read: "Philip, one of the twelve who sleeps in Hierapolis, and his two aged virgin daughters. Another of his daughters, who lived in the Holy Spirit, rests at Ephesus."

HOLY MARTYRS

At the close of Book 8, in the *Book of Martyrs,* chapter 11, we read concerning Porphyry,

> Truly filled with the Spirit, and covered with his philosophical garb thrown around him like a cloak, and with a calm and composed mind giving exhortations and beckoning to his acquaintances and friends, he preserved a cheerful countenance at the very stake.

A little later in the same chapter he records the death of another martyr who was filled with the Holy Spirit.

> Julianus had just come from abroad, and not yet entered the city, when learning of the death of the martyrs on the road, he immediately hastened to the sight. There, when he saw the earthly tabernacles of the holy men lying on the ground, he embraced each one, and kissed them all. Upon this he was immediately seized by the ministers of

death, and conducted to Firmilianus, who consigned him to a slow, lingering fire. Then Julianus, also, leaping and exulting with joy, gave thanks to God with a loud voice, who had honored him with a martyr's death. He also was a native of Cappadocia, but in his manner he was most religious, and eminent for the sincerity and soundness of his faith. He was also devoted in other respects, and animated by the Holy Spirit himself.

In Book 8, chapter 7, Eusebius calls those who suffered for Christ at Phenice holy:

At these scenes we have been present ourselves, when we also observed the divine power of our Lord and Saviour, Jesus Christ himself present, and effectually displayed in them; when for a long time the devouring wild beasts would not dare either touch or to approach the bodies of those pious men, but directed their violence against others. But they would not even touch the holy wrestlers standing and striking at them with their hands as they were commanded, in order to irritate the beasts against them. Sometimes, indeed, they would also rush upon them, but, as if repulsed by some divine power, they again retreated. This continued for a long time, creating no little wonder to the spectators; so that now again on account of the failure in the first instance, they were obliged to let loose the beasts a second and a third time upon one and the same martyr. One could not help being astonished at the intrepid perseverance of these holy men, and the firm and invincible mind of these also, whose bodies were young and tender. For you could see a youth of scarcely twenty years, standing unbound, with his arms extended like a cross, but with an intrepid and fearless earnestness, intensely engaged in prayer to God, neither removing nor declining from the spot where he stood, whilst bears and leopards breathed rage and death, almost touching his very flesh, and yet I know not how, by a divine power, they had their mouths in a manner bridled, and again retreated in haste.

CHAPTER FOURTEEN

Holiness Through All Ages of the Church

HOLINESS is one of the highest attributes of God. Man was created in His image, not the physical image, but in His moral likeness. "Which after God is created in righteousness and true holiness" (Eph. 4:24). Man lost his blessed holy estate by the fall, but the new man may be restored again to holiness through the merits of our Saviour. The first thing that God did to set man an example was to rest upon the Sabbath day; He sanctified it and made it holy. God not only created man in His image of holiness, but He wishes man to be like Him through all the ages. "Be ye holy; for I am holy" (I Peter 1:16).

God would not permit Moses to approach Him without first recognizing His holiness. The Holy Spirit anointed the judges and kings of Israel. Samuel anointed David with oil, and the Spirit of the Lord came upon him from that day forward (I Samuel 16:13). The prophets were moved and spake by the Spirit. Isaiah was only a man of unclean lips until God touched him with the fire and Holy Spirit. John the Baptist had a special anointing of the Holy Ghost, and so did Jesus. The apostles received the outpouring of the Holy Spirit on the Day of Pentecost; and time and time again the Holy Spirit came upon them with fresh power in times of need.

The birthday of the Church was a baptism of the Holy Ghost, and this same power has been found in the Church ever since. Sometimes only a few have professed it, but God never has been without a witness of holiness in the earth. Paul was constantly talking about it. When the Church needed to select officers, the qualification for deacons was "men of honest report, full of the Holy Ghost and wisdom." When new converts believed, as at Ephesus, the Church sent down certain disciples, who inquired, "Have ye received the Holy Ghost since ye believed?" And when they heard that they had not, they laid their hands on them, and "they were baptized in the name of the Lord Jesus."

Great Bible scholars and church historians recognize the fact that it was the custom of the Early Church to pray for all believers to be filled with the Spirit. The usual custom was to baptize the converts, and then the elders would lay their hands upon them and pray that they might receive the gift of the Holy Ghost. The Early Church believed in and prayed for the filling of the Holy Spirit, and this was the secret of their great power. They lived in the Spirit, walked in the Spirit, prayed in the Spirit, and testified in the Spirit. They were undaunted in persecution because they were helped by the Holy Spirit within them.

Many writers before the days of Constantine have left their testimony that they believed in and lived a life of holiness; from some of these we have quoted. The same thing is seen in the literature coming from Ambrose, Chrysostom, Jerome, and Augustine. When the Church became ritualistic and formal, the Latins demanded four-score pounds of gold for the anointing oil, and there was a quarrel between the Roman and the Greek Catholic churches. The Greeks rejected the authority of the Roman bishop, and began to consecrate their own anointing oil; and since that time they have been separate churches.

From time to time through the Dark Ages witnesses to the truth of holiness appeared, and with the dawn of the Reformation the light begins to shine again. The Quietist movement among the Roman Catholics, which centered around Fenelon and Madame Guyon, and the Quakers among the Protestants, were two great movements to make the whole Church feel the need of being filled with and led by the Holy Spirit.

John Calvin acknowledged that the custom of praying for the new converts to be filled with the Holy Ghost was derived from the apostles, and admitted that the Protestants should have something in the place of it, yet did not emphasize this in his teachings. We read this from his "Commentaries" when commenting on Hebrews 6:2, which speaks of laying on of hands:

> This one passage abundantly testifies that this rite had its beginning from the Apostles, which afterwards, however, was turned into superstition, as the world almost always degenerates into corruption. . . . . Wherefore the pure institution at this day ought to be retained, but the superstition ought to be removed.

In Oxford University there was a group of students who were seeking after holiness; they were ridiculed and called the "Holy Club." Soon we hear of the great Wesley revival which was conducted by some of the former members of this club. They placed great emphasis upon the Holy Spirit and the doctrine of sanctification. Wesley said that the purpose of the Methodist church was to spread scriptural holiness over the lands. He says in his *Journal* that at one time there were almost as many people seeking and claiming entire sanctification as claimed salvation in his meetings. When the movement spread to America, hundreds and thousands were reached. Many were professing the blessing of holiness for many years in the Methodist meetings, especially in the revival and camp meetings. Then the modern holiness movement began to be heard of; at first it was interdemoninational. Those who believed in and professed the experience of holiness, from all churches, began to get together in associations and hold revivals and camp meetings all over America, and also in other countries.

As opposition became more and more marked, it soon became evident that, if the cause of holiness was to be conserved, it would be necessary to organize the work. Then little holiness churches began to appear in the eastern part of our country, and almost simultaneously they appeared on the western coast, and in the South. Several of these churches united under the leadership of Dr. P. F. Bresee and Dr. H. F. Reynolds, and the Church of the Nazarene came into existence in 1908. Other holiness churches appeared, and thousands now belong to the holiness churches. Hundreds of young people are in the holiness colleges, and other holiness institutions are aiding in various capacities to carry on the work. Thousands of pages of holiness literature are coming from the presses of the publishing houses of those who believe in holiness. Holiness churches and revival meetings dot the land from coast to coast where the holy fire burns upon the altar; and sacrificing missionaries are carrying the message of full salvation to the ends of the earth.

The long list of the holy saints of God who have lived and preached holiness is too numerous to mention, but God has them all recorded in the Book of Life. The apostles carried the message of holiness from the Upper Room on the Day of Pentecost to the Jews, and Paul was not satisfied until he had carried the same truth to almost all the great Gentile cities. John laid down the work at Ephesus at the close of the first Christian century; then the long stream of heroes carried the same truth to the multitudes from that day to this.

There are Polycarp, Clement, Barnabas, and Hermas of the early days of the Church, preaching the truth. Ambrose, Athanasius, and Chrysostom followed the days of Constantine with the blessed, holy gospel; and a few lights here and there shined out from the Dark Ages with the message of holiness. Savonarola thundered against sin and worldliness in the streets of cultured Florence until the people knew that they must live holy lives. One of the vilest popes had him burned on the public square of the city he had done so much for and loved so dearly. Fenelon and Madame Guyon were bright lights for holiness among the Catholics.

Then there are George Fox, John and Charles Wesley, George Whitefield, and John Fletcher in England. There are Jonathan and Mrs. Edwards, David Brainerd, and Asbury, who enjoyed the blessing of holiness in the early history of America; they are followed by Upham, Mahan, Charles Finney, the great revivalist who preached holiness. And we may mention Harriet Beecher Stowe, Mrs. Phoebe Palmer, Frances Ridley Havergal, Frances Willard, and Hannah Whitall Smith, who wrote *The Christian's Secret of a Happy Life,* and a host of others from among the noble women who enjoyed the blessing of holiness. Then there are A. B. Simpson, David Updegraff, Daniel Steele of Boston University, J. A. Wood, Inskip, and McDonald, all great holiness preachers; and on down to our sainted Dr. P. F. Bresee—these all died in the faith.

Today, hundreds are preaching the same message of holiness to the masses; almost everywhere you go there is an advocate of holiness. Who has not heard of the late Bud Robinson, who for so many years preached holiness every time he spoke?

THE CHURCH OF THE NAZARENE AND HOLINESS

The fight for holiness did not originate in the twentieth century, nor with the Church of the Nazarene. No, it is the fight of the ages. Holiness graced the inner chambers of eternity. Holiness is older than sin; it is coexistent with God. Holiness is as eternal as the Jehovah of the Bible. "For thus saith the high and lofty One that inhabiteth eternity, whose name is Holy; I dwell in the high and holy place, with him also that is of a contrite and humble spirit" (Isa. 57:15). We may be accused of being a small bunch of religious "faddists" with a new notion of religion that we are trying to propagate, but not so. Those who judge us so are only betraying their own ignorance and lack of reading concerning holiness, sanctification, and perfect love. We are not alone. The greatest minds and holiest saints of all ages of the Christian Church have upheld the doctrine and enjoyed the experience of holiness.

Holiness is not just a doctrine of the Church of the Nazarene held by a little handful of professors of religion here and there, but there are a great number from almost all denominations who believe in and teach the same blessed truth of holiness. There is a great cloud of witnesses to the rich experience that the children of God may enjoy. A number of denominations are known as holiness churches. The Methodist church stood for holiness before she grew so worldly and filled with Modernism. Some teaching on holiness occurs in the doctrines of almost every church. The Wesleyan Methodists, Free Methodists, Primitive Methodists, Orthodox Quakers, Holiness Methodists, Reformed Baptists, Full Gospel Presbyterians, Christian Missionary Alliance, Pilgrim Holiness, Salvation Army, and a number of smaller churches stand with the Church of the Nazarene as advocates of holiness.

Its Doctrine of Holiness

The Church of the Nazarene stands for the fundamental evangelical doctrines, but makes the test of all its standard of holiness and entire sanctification. The doctrine of the church on entire sanctification or holiness is as follows:

> 10. We believe that entire sanctification is that act of God, subsequent to regeneration, by which believers are made free from original sin, or depravity, and brought into a state of entire devotement to God, and the holy obedience of love made perfect.

It is wrought by the baptism with the Holy Spirit, and comprehends in one experience the cleansing of the heart from sin and the abiding indwelling presence of the Holy Spirit, empowering the believer for life and service.

Entire sanctification is provided by the blood of Jesus, is wrought instantaneously by faith, preceded by entire consecration; and to this work and state of grace the Holy Spirit bears witness.

This experience is also known by various terms representing its different phases, such as "Christian Perfection," "Perfect Love," "Heart Purity," "The Baptism with the Holy Spirit," "The Fullness of the Blessing," and "Christian Holiness."—*Manual*, Church of the Nazarene.

We'll girdle the globe with salvation,
With holiness unto the Lord . . . .

Reader, do you enjoy this blessing? It may be yours today.